# MARKETING STRATEGY

for

Peter Maple

Institute of
Fundraising

**The fundraising series**
*Community Fundraising* Harry Brown (editor)
*Corporate Fundraising* Valerie Morton (editor)
*Fundraising Databases* Peter Flory
*Fundraising Strategy* Redmond Mullin
*Legacy Fundraising* Sebastian Wilberforce (editor)
*Marketing Strategy* Peter Maple
*Trust Fundraising* Anthony Clay (editor)

First published 2003

Copyright © Directory of Social Change 2003

Published by:
Directory of Social Change          Tel. 020 7209 5151
24 Stephenson Way                   Fax 020 7391 4804
London                              e-mail: books@dsc.org.uk
NW1 2DP                             www.dsc.org.uk
from whom further copies and a full publications list are available.

The Directory of Social Change is a Registered Charity no. 800517

Text and cover design by Eugenie Dodd Typographics
Typeset by Tradespools, Frome
Printed and bound by Bell & Bain Ltd, Glasgow

A catalogue record for this book is available from the British Library

ISBN 1 903991 38 2

# Contents

# Acknowledgements

Firstly I want to acknowledge the huge contribution of Stephen Elsden to this book. Without his energy, enthusiasm and perseverance this work would never have seen the light of day. Stephen's input to the original proposal was crucial to its success and he helped enormously with the first few chapters. Also a massive thank you to Alison Baxter my publisher; her guidance and forbearance when early deadlines were missed helped me to refocus and produce what, I hope, readers will perceive as a more complete, useful guide to the subject matter.

Most important of all for me has been the support of my partner Norma who is not only a consummate psychotherapist but gave me vital reality checks on the text at key moments. Her proof reading of early drafts and helpful feedback ensured that the text is, I believe, very accessible.

However without the insights of the many named and anonymous contributors who I interviewed this would be a very dry theoretical tome. To everyone who has helped and encouraged me in the production of the book, thank you.

Individually I would like to thank and pay tribute to: Richard Gutch, Kate Nash, Simon Burne, Stephen Pidgeon, Jeremy Prescott, Tony Cram, Mark Astarita, Howard Lake, Jeremy Hughes, Simon Collings, Judy Beard, Adrian Sargeant, Jo Saxton, Andrew Hope, David Saint, Redmond Mullin, Steve Andrews, Paul Amadi, Catherine Lightfoot, Myra Bennett, John Tomlinson, Tony Mainwaring, Verity Haines, Andrew Watts, Mike Baker, Teresa Dauncey, Tony Elisher, and to those I have forgotton to mention but who have also inspired and helped me, sorry and thank you

In particular I need to thank, for allowing me to reproduce text, pictures, charts and advertisements the following organisations: Amnesty International, The Giving Campaign, Remember a Charity, Crossbow, Citigate Albert Frank, Brooke Hospital for Animals, Diabetes UK, Oxfam, Target Direct, Whitewater, Mcmillan Cancer Relief, British Red Cross and Barnardo's

And in addition I should also thank:

Acorns Hospice, Arthritis Care, BackCare, British Lung Foundation, CAFOD, Cancer Research UK, Cards for Good Causes, Central School of Speech and Drama, English Hockey, Great Ormond Street Hospital, Institute of Fundraising, Jewish Care, Leonard Cheshire, Mcmillan Cancer Relief, National Deaf Children's Society, Oxfam, RADAR, RNLI, Sense, Sue Ryder Care, Ryder Cheshire, YMCA, Ashridge Management Centre, nfp Synergy (Future Foundation), HSBC, Apple Computers, Optimedia, Smee & Ford, Fundraising.co.uk

# CHAPTER ONE

# Why charities need marketing and marketing needs charities

'Marketing provides a philosophy as well as a planning mechanism.'

*Ian Bruce*

'There's always a better deal to be had.'       *Chester Karass*

This chapter examines the context in which charities operate today. For-profit and not-for-profit marketing practices are contrasted and the benefits of each learning from the other are considered. Importantly this chapter aims to show that whilst charities have a great need to adopt effective integrated commercial marketing practices, for-profit organisations ignore the best of what charity marketing offers at their peril.

## Perspectives

The advent of active fundraising in the UK can be dated back at least to the eleventh century. Marketing is a rather younger concept for both commercial and voluntary organisations, but its importance to fundraising in the voluntary sector, including even the smallest of charities, has perhaps never been as great.

There is no single reason for this; marketing has not been imposed out of the blue on an unsuspecting industry, but as the voluntary sector has developed it has become aware of the benefits that marketing strategy, plans and initiatives can bring in meeting the challenges faced by not-for-profits today. Whilst the language of marketing may not always come easily to many operating in the sector, the strategy and practices that it imposes are crucial to the success of not-for-profit organisations. Joe Saxton (2002) who is the 'driver of ideas' for the Future Foundation says, 'if the word brand grates then mentally replace it with the word image or reputation'. This advice, if followed, could help many trustees and volunteers begin to understand just how much value is 'locked-up' within the name and reputation of a well known national organisation. Chapter four will look in depth at brand issues, particularly as they relate to charities.

# Some definitions

**FIGURE 1** INTERLOCKING CIRCLES OF PUBLIC, PRIVATE AND VOLUNTARY ORGANISATIONAL ACTIVITY

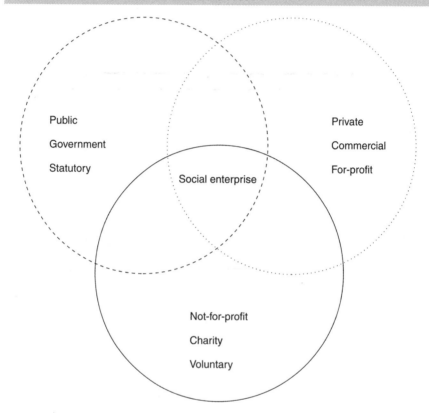

As Figure 1 shows, public, private and voluntary sectors can be thought of in a number of ways and there is considerable overlap in their spheres of operation. Recent comment characterises community action network organisations as hybrids between private and public sectors, or voluntary and private sectors; they can therefore best be thought of as the overlapping area in the middle. This area is capable of very significant growth and Chapter seven offers further comment.

Classic text book definitions of marketing range from 'meeting customer needs' to 'the identification of consumer demand and the design through to delivery of satisfactory product in a profitable manner'. Every definition has the common elements of delivering satisfaction whilst maintaining a sustainable business.

Charities might argue that their particular role, to change the world, is inimical to this business ethos. However given that every established charity recognises that the problems it seeks to address are, by definition, intractable, complex and long term, there is an equal argument in favour of considering how good commercial practices might be successfully applied to the task. Philip Kotler's definition, developed in the 1970s and aimed principally at service providers, still fits the bill rather well for not-for-profit organisations. He said: 'Marketing is the analysis, planning, implementation and control of carefully formulated programmes designed to bring about voluntary exchanges of values with target markets to achieve institutional objectives' (Kotler and Fox 1985).

The *Dictionary of Business* (1996) defines marketing more succinctly as 'the process of planning and executing the conception, pricing, promotion, and distribution of ideas, products, and services to create exchanges that will satisfy the needs of individuals and organisations'.

It is important to note that many aspects of marketing that have been developed successfully by charities are ignored by commercial organisations at their peril. A main argument of this book is that the two sectors still have much to learn from one another. Whilst commercial marketing models may not always transplant successfully into not-for-profit organisations, it is certain that many good marketing practices, integrated and well understood by all who must contribute, will be enormously beneficial to those charities which successfully adopt them. The flow-back into for-profit organisations will equally, it is contended, produce strong marketing advantages.

# Consider the competition

The for-profit or commercial sector has embraced an integrated approach to marketing for decades. Indeed from global players like HSBC to sole traders, the requirement to differentiate and meet customer need in competition with other providers has meant that marketing considerations permeate organisations both vertically and horizontally. That is, good marketing planning tends to work from the board right down to the newest trainees and across functions including production, distribution, administration and human resources. A service provider like HSBC is interesting in its approach to its reputation and the case study quoted in Chapter two goes into more detail about this.

*people chose*
*charities* ✓
*to support*

In the voluntary sector, which encompasses in the UK more than 185,000 registered charities (Charity Commission 2002) and up to 600,000 similar organisations (Mawson 2002), competition between not-for-profits is inevitable. Should a prospective donor want to support a cancer charity, they can choose Mcmillan Cancer Relief, Marie Curie, Cancer Research UK, Breakthrough Breast Cancer, BACUP, and hundreds more national and smaller, local organisations. Even making a second-level choice to give just to a cancer care organisation, or a charity focused on a specific cancer, leaves a large number of possible candidates for support.

If our hypothetical donor's interest is in children's charities, the choice can seem equally bewildering. The first to be formed, The Thomas Coram Foundation (for (foundling babies) actually dates back to 1739 and is still going strong. Dr Barnardo's, National Children's Homes, The Children's Society and the NSPCC were all founded within a few years of each other in the nineteenth century, each from a different religious basis. Now these five organisations, some using new names, co-exist alongside a further 22,346 registered children's charities (Charity Commission 2002). A similar situation exists for disability charities, medical research, animal protection, and just about any other 'cause' a donor wishes to choose.

It is perhaps natural that charities should diversify and propagate themselves. A national organisation may be founded to address a major illness, such as multiple sclerosis. It will soon experience a range of demands from those who live with, or in the shadow of this condition – for research into a cure, for respite and care support, for self-help groups, for information on accessible lifestyles – and these demands will themselves be replicated at a local level. Only the strongest and wealthiest of organisations can effectively address such a range of demands. The most likely model is for local, specialist charities to be established, supporting for example self-help groups in the north east of England, and these smaller niche charities are as likely to be independent of a national organisation as they are to operate under its wider umbrella.

Such a scenario has been played out time and again.

A more recent trend, however, is for unification of charities. These range from the merger several years ago of a number of charities for the visually impaired under the umbrella organisation Action for Blind People, to the more recent merger of numerous HIV and AIDS charities with the far better known Terrence Higgins Trust. This particular charity has continued to prosper in the face of declining fortunes for many AIDS support organisations and has taken on the mantels of those who would otherwise have been compelled to close due to changes in funding or need (or both). In addition the very important combination of national charity giants Imperial Cancer Research Fund and Cancer Research Campaign to produce Cancer Research UK is perhaps a portent of many more mergers to come.

## CASE STUDY **CANCER RESEARCH UK**

Talks about a possible merger between these two giants (both had turnovers in excess of £100 million) date back to 1980. A merger was finally agreed and the new charity came into existence in July 2002. An important factor for both boards of trustees was, after much analysis of respective supporter databases, a firm belief that, overall, greater net funding for cancer research could be generated by a single merged operation.

Peter Vickery-Smith, director of marketing and fundraising at CRUK, argues that cross-sector partnerships and campaigns often become confused and can lead to mismanagement. He believes that 'charities need to be brave enough to take the extra step'. His view of the ICRF and CRC merger is that it has led to increased flexibility and improved service delivery. He feels that charities must acknowledge that the increasingly saturated marketplace could pose real threats to the continuing health of the voluntary sector and that more charities should therefore consider merging to increase public confidence in the sector.

Despite this, the landscape of the voluntary sector is still made up of many thousands of similar organisations competing for funds, volunteers and service users. Moreover 5,000 new ones are being formed and registered each year.

Merger is, of course, only one avenue of cooperation and other less final solutions are open to those wishing to solve particular marketing problems. Assisi is a payroll giving consortium formed by 11 animal-oriented charities to promote and develop employee support thorough payroll donations. Many of the collaborating partners are very small with little public profile, and so workplace canvassing would be unlikely to prove cost effective for them. Assisi has been enormously successful in acting as a single point of reference for those interested in helping animals via salary deductions, so much so that it has now been constituted as a charity in its own right, with the remit to raise funds for the member charities. There are also moves amongst other groups of charities to share back office facilities, and to take advantage of group purchasing schemes in order to reduce costs and to improve effectiveness. Similarly, Four Cs and Cards for Good Causes have had success in the charity Christmas card market.

CASE STUDY **CARDS FOR GOOD CAUSES (CFGC)**

Founder and ex chief executive of CFGC Judith Rich says, 'the initial impetus to provide better distribution for the member charities just grew and grew'. When Rich arrived in 1976 there were just 17 charities loosely co-operating as the '1959 group' over cards in one another's own charity shops. With Rich's drive, enthusiasm and determination the consortium never looked back.

Independent outlets, temporary shops in halls, churches and empty shops are secured each year. Central warehousing for participating charitys' cards has been introduced and the numbers of 'guest charities' participating in selected shops in return for providing volunteers to help staff those shops has increased dramatically.

During the 1999 Christmas season 296 charities had cards sold through nearly 300 retail outlets raising almost £6 million for the participants.

For individual charities marketing is, however, essential: to differentiate one charity from another and to help identify and sell the unique proposition of any organisation. This might be that a charity operates in Newcastle as opposed to another that only serves the Manchester area, or that one organisation provides information to the public as opposed to another that campaigns for change by local or national government. Only by stressing its USP – unique selling proposition – can any charity expect to gain competitive advantage, and as this chapter will further explain, a myriad of other external pressures mean that many not-for-profits without a competitive advantage will be doomed to fail in the twenty-first century. Provided that this lead to mergers with net resulting increases for benificiaries this pressure could be a very positive one. The danger remains however that volunteer trustees become discouraged, closure results and the net impact is a reduction in services offered.

Higher education establishments are an interesting case. As not-for-profit organisations, fee- and grant-driven but often with large development departments to generate additional voluntary income for capital projects, they are well placed to integrate marketing through those development functions. After all they are looking to the future of the establishment – what research, course development and future services the organisation will offer and how strategically it will deliver those services (in short the full marketing mix). All too often however universities and schools accept their brand as given and simply regard development as the means to this end. This is perhaps where such establishments differ from high profile, cause-based charities. Many educational establishments rely on differentiating themselves and pursuing excellence only in particular niches. Yet they have the ability, when they choose to use it, to harness marketing to drive development and fuel the future.

For example the Central School of Speech and Drama in London has very clear, well stated aims to, 'reach out, promoting excellence and building on a reputation that is already second to none' says their new development director Verity Haines, She sees the need to 'line all the soldiers up' before going public with any fundraising activity. She adds, ' the school has a unique opportunity to market its future courses at a world-wide audience. But it'll only work if through good marketing, we've established who those potential attendees are and how we talk to them effectively.' She sees that the school could work independently, but collaborate with other organisations that might otherwise be seen as competitors.

Even in the area of higher education, however, mergers are not only a theoretical option to maximise growth and competitiveness but are actually happening amongst some of the major players. In March 2002, Manchester University and UMIST announced plans to merge and become Britain's largest university with up to 28,000 full-time students. In August London Guildhall and UNL (University of North London) merged to form the London Metropolitan University with up to 25,000 students.

Perhaps most surprising of all is the proposed merger of Imperial College and University College London (UCL). UCL already faces well-publicised financial deficits and Dr Chris Towler, Imperial's director of strategy and development admitted that whist the universities already collaborate in many ways they are currently forced to compete for research funding. The hope is that as a giant international player with a turnover of more than £800 million the new institution will attract more research funding than traditional competitors. It is hoped that it will be constituted and open for business by the summer of 2004, and would top the research league in the UK.

# Issues of public confidence

The mergers outlined above are but one consequence of a growing suspicion among the British public – that not-for-profit groups are no longer the blameless, efficient organisations they were once assumed to be. High profile scandals involving the misappropriation and misuse of funds, 'big business' marketing and fundraising techniques and a general cynicism in the media where 'good news' stories are no longer of interest have all conspired to reduce public confidence in the not-for-profit and voluntary sector.

Against this background, not-for-profits are being forced to become more transparent about their operations and their respective costs, explaining why investment in fundraising and promotion is essential if organisations are to survive and continue to serve the individuals and groups who have come to rely on them. This requires a greater understanding of the public's attitudes and concerns, so that appropriate marketing and communication strategies can be developed. Increasingly, not-for-profits and charities are signing up to specialist omnibus surveys, such as those offered by Fund Ratios and The Charity Monitor, to check and understand the changing landscape of public attitudes, behaviour and perceptions.

There is also the supposed phenomenon of 'donor fatigue'. Opinion is divided as to whether this is a real or purely theoretical phenomenon. It is, perhaps, most likely that people are simply tired of being asked repeatedly and inappropriately. Nevertheless recent years have seen the overall value of donations to UK charities stagnating, and the advent of the National Lottery cannot be totally to blame. The public is not diverting its donations out of individual charities and into the Lottery or other umbrella appeals. The money normally given is being diverted into expenditure on homes, on entertainment and holidays, and increasingly on the cost of care for parents and grandparents in later life. This is perhaps evidenced by the serious downturn in the value of charitable legacies seen by a number of charities in the last few years.

Only by reminding the public that charitable giving is a vital element of modern society can fundraising organisations hope to expand the overall pot of money available to not-for-profit groups. Without that, charities will be forced to 'rob Peter to pay Paul', fighting among themselves for dwindling financial resources. There have been attempts in the past to run generic marketing campaigns promoting the 'giving is good' message, (including the doomed 'Windsor campaign') and further work in this area is already underway.

An initiative has been spearheaded by the National Council for Voluntary Organisation (NCVO) and the Institute of Fundraising: the 'Giving Campaign' is the result of this work. And whilst its rebranding of Gift Aid can only assist public awareness, whether the overall campaign will have a marked effect on levels of charitable giving remains to be seen. A more detailed discussion of this and the linked legacy campaign follows in Chapter seven.

# Taking on the private sector

It would be wholly wrong to suggest that competition for charities can come only from other fundraising and voluntary organisations. A large number of charities are involved in the delivery of direct services to the elderly, to disabled people, those with terminal illnesses, animals, and other groups. Leonard Cheshire, for example, delivers respite care, domiciliary services, day centre places, long-term residential care and employment services. Many of these services are delivered under contract with local Social Services Departments, and there are many other not-for-profit and for-profit organisations delivering similar services and competing for the same contracts in many areas of the UK.

Not only does this mean that 'unique selling propositions' (USPs) must again come into play, but charities must also adapt their practices to meet the strict requirements levied by local government departments. It is a fallacy to believe that contracts are awarded on price alone (see Chapter three), although this is certainly a very significant factor and one that some charities are struggling to cope with. The way in which an organisation's services – its products – are packaged and presented is critical in securing a successful partnership with the public sector, and it is equally important that any competing charity understands the requirements and demands of its client. When tendering for contracts, it is important to remember that at that particular point in time, the client is the body offering the contract, not the individual user who will ultimately receive the service.

Quality and standards are vitally important here, values which, when clearly in evidence, can be powerful marketing tools. Services must be properly monitored and evaluated, ensuring that the requirements of contractors are continually met, if not exceeded. This also demands a regular dialogue with the contracting organisation and with service users or their families, if the charity is to deliver on all expectations. Contracts always come with a renewal date, and a charity that forgets this, and allows a service, once awarded, to decline, will almost inevitably lose the contract the next time around. As in any area in which it is employed, marketing must be seen as a long-term exercise, not a short-term fix.

# Keeping the customer satisfied

In the previous section, emphasis was given to considering the needs of the contractor of a charitable service, over and above those of the eventual recipient of that service. However, end-users, whether customers or donors, are as important for not-for-profit organisations as they are for commercial retailers and other sales and marketing driven companies. It therefore follows that, as the voluntary sector expands and becomes more competitive, the requirements of these end-users must be taken into full account.

The concept of 'relationship fundraising' is no longer new to charities, and in fact has been practised by some organisations for many years. As long ago as the early 1990s, Barnardo's wrote to all of its regular direct mail donors, and asked them how often they would like to hear from the charity each year. By treating its donors as individuals, Barnardo's successfully reduced unwanted direct mail, saving on costs, and saw a corresponding uplift in the value of donations from its grateful supporters. This followed some pioneering work by Lawrence Stroud on behalf of Botton Village, a community of people with severe learning difficulties. Addressing a workshop at the National Fundraising Convention in Birmingham (1995), Stroud made the point that, by consistently asking donors what information they wanted and how often they wanted it, the charity enjoyed remarkable response rates from the donor database. Other organisations – such as Greenpeace and the NSPCC – have followed suit, asking their supporters what it is they want to know, and tailoring their approaches and communications accordingly.

Supermarkets and banks are increasingly using these same relationship marketing techniques, and the discerning member of the public is coming to expect to be treated as an individual, rather than just an entry on a database. There are further benefits also to the charity, in that it costs far more to recruit a new donor than it does to service an existing supporter and keep them loyal to the organisation. Whilst a new donor, recruited through what is probably at best a break-even cold mailing and more usually a very significant investment, may become a valuable supporter over time, existing donors can provide a more immediate financial return if treated correctly.

There is, however, a limit to the extent to which any charity can call a supporter 'its own'. What has become evident in recent years is that donor loyalty does not mean donor monogamy. Many individuals will support a basket of charities, perhaps giving a regular amount to two or three, and more occasional donations to several others. The same phenomenon can be seen in individual's retailing habits, where stores are chosen depending on their current offers and availability, and consumers boast of a number of 'store cards' in their wallets and purses. Indeed the latest response to this 'customer promiscuity' is for some of the major players to issue a joint loyalty, or bonus card called Nectar. Even on the Internet, few if any websites have the exclusive attention of surfers, though individuals may choose from a selection of personally selected favourites. When a charity's closest supporters may also be making donations to indirect, if not direct, competitors, principles of customer care are vitally important if individuals are not to take their business, and their donations, entirely elsewhere.

Interestingly, opportunities abound wherever there is change. The 2001 census reveals that the population is ageing rapidly. This is clearly a marketing opportunity for companies aiming products and services at older people. Not-for-profits directing services at the elderly will see increasing demands upon their resources. But where are the joint ventures to fund such growth? For example various attempts have been made to establish lists of reputable plumbers and builders for vulnerable people living alone (or indeed anyone desperate for a reliable service) but endorsement by a charity working directly with older people would enormously enhance the reputation and brand of such a service provider. British Gas has attempted to tap into this market by advertising central heating maintenance contracts in the style of emergency medical assistance but the linked programmes are conspicuous by their absence.

# Making staff and volunteers matter

This competition for individuals doesn't just focus on donors and other fundraising supporters, or on those bodies that contract for charitable services. Another story of dwindling resources and increased competition can be told of staff and volunteer recruitment, where many organisations, both large and small, face crisis. This is particularly true for those charities whose 'people' are responsible for delivering services, as opposed to fundraising or more administrative support.

There are a number of reasons for this. In terms of recruiting staff, charities are always up against commercial organisations that can pay higher salaries and offer more attractive benefits in terms of paid holiday, health insurance and pension contributions. This is less of a problem when recruiting specialist staff, such as fundraisers, as the competition is only between charities and other organisations involved in that area. But when recruiting care staff, and those with the management expertise to oversee them, there are always commercial providers seeking similarly strong candidates to fill these posts, and in such situations the perks and benefits on offer can often influence a candidtate's decision.

An inherent advantage for charities, which a good marketing strategy can help to exploit, is their closeness to the individuals they serve. This is not to suggest that commercial providers are only out to make a profit – although this has to be the principal factor for them – but charities have a unique understanding of the needs of their service users. More forward-thinking charities are placing service user representatives on their trustee boards and in other positions at the top of their organisation. This empathy with the needs of service users can help to inspire and motivate existing staff, and also attract new staff, drawn to a career in service delivery because of their beliefs – and there are few individuals who would seek a job in the third sector for the money alone.

Empathy is even more important when recruiting volunteers, who are not driven at all by financial gain but instead may wish to give something back to the community in which they have prospered, or to develop new skills they are unable to practise in their regular paid employment. As with donors, volunteers are also faced with a bewildering choice of charities to which they can give their time, and any organisation must work hard to understand what prospective volunteers are seeking, and to match those needs with what the charity itself can offer. Competition here comes not just from other charities. Any individual with time to spare has a number of opportunities before them – taking up a new hobby, fitting in freelance work, spending more time with their family, among other options – so it is certainly not a given that volunteering is top of their list. But with an effective marketing campaign, charities can both raise awareness of volunteering *per se*, and specifically volunteering opportunities within their own organisation.

Equally, commercial organisations with training, team development and morale building priorities ignore the lessons of working with voluntary organisations at their peril. Examples of coordinated staff volunteering abound, as do the reports of improved team working, job satisfaction and increased productivity. Marks & Spencer for example actively encourage staff working singly or in small teams to spend time as volunteers working on a wide range of community projects. They report significant successes from both employer and employee perspectives.

The positive encouragement by B&Q of the employment of older and disabled staff has resulted directly in greater employee loyalty, particularly at a local level where a team spirit can be significantly enhanced. Staff turnover has fallen and morale has been improved. An additional benefit from this has been an increase in staff volunteering projects, perhaps because of the wider existing community involvement of those older staff members.

In a similar way charities can use staff to achieve multiple objectives. For example they can augment fundraising activities and at
the same time build internal understanding of those very fundraising needs. An instance here is when a number of non-fund-
raising staff at Leonard Cheshire took part in an overseas challenge
event to 'walk the volcanoes' in Nicaragua and succeeded in raising
several thousand pounds of additional income for overseas projects.
Importantly however they also built greater internal understanding
of the fundraising needs and priorities in an organisation that
employs 7,000 staff mostly on the service delivery side. Shared values and greater understanding were the end result. The beneficial
effects upon the organisations that adopt such practices can reach
much further and multiply when such activities bring together two
non-competitive organisations: Tesco adopted Mencap for the year
and 200 staff accompanied Mencap's fundraisers on a specially
organised overseas challenge. This emphasis on people can enable
a corporate to achieve benefits from working with a charity that
extend far beyond those of simple altruism and philanthropy.

CASE STUDY **THE MITIE GROUP AND MCMILLAN CANCER RELIEF**

The Mitie Group is a very disparate group of some 64 companies
providing facilities management around the UK. Whilst enjoying highly
profitable growth, Mitie was experiencing significant internal
communications problems and a lack of staff involvement with or
ownership of the group's overall objectives. However Mitie experienced
huge success with its adoption of Mcmillan Cancer over the two years
1998 and 1999. Working closely with the Mitie's human resources team
Mcmillan Cancer organised a nationwide series of bowling competitions,
pitting Mitie group companies and teams against one another. As well as
being the main fundraising vehicle the competitions achieved huge
improvements in inter-company knowledge and staff morale. These
benefits, to paraphrase John Urquhart (corporate relations director of the
Mitie Group plc) could not have happened without the charity's
involvement. This demonstrates clearly the win–win possibilities of a
successful joint venture when communications and marketing objectives
are clearly understood by both participants.

# Conclusion

Commercial organisations tend to plan marketing as an integrated
part of their overall strategy; brand development fits into this tight
framework and the resulting plans dovetail neatly together even if
they don't always work. By contrast charities tend to act in a more

*ad hoc* way, adding marketing to the fundraising and communications function so that plans are added almost as an afterthought. Even where rigorous planning is executed, in some of the larger not-for-profits marketing considerations tend to follow the communications strategy rather than dictate them.

It is clear from the examples mentioned above that for-profit organisations can benefit hugely from cooperation with not-for-profit organisations and similarly not-for-profits can benefit over and above the obvious fundraising objectives.

Commercial organisations are learning that competitive advantage can be gained by directing marketing effort – not just community affairs budgets – towards active work with charities. Benefits accrue both internally and externally. Internally from better communications and morale, reduced staff turnover and more productive teams with higher loyalty and championing of the brand. Externally customers identify more closely with a favourable brand and may be more loyal whilst other stakeholders such as investors are equally likely to be more favourably disposed. In turn not-for-profit organisations are beginning to understand the need to consider their own marketing priorities when building strategic plans, as opposed to grafting marketing activities onto existing fundraising programmes. There is however much more that can be done on both sides.

# CHAPTER TWO

# A brief history of marketing

'No boy will ever be refused admission.'          *Dr Barnardo*

'Half the money I spend on advertising is wasted, and the trouble is I don't know which half.'          *Viscount Leverhulme*

Looking back over the twentieth century (and, in a few relevant instances, earlier) this chapter explores how charities in particular have increasingly come to rely on marketing methods and practice, drawing direct parallels with successful commercial marketeers through the decades. Beginning with some of the early pioneering work of Barnardo's and later Oxfam, it will show how marketing has evolved into today's practice and begins to show how it might go so much further.

Inevitably this chapter and chapter three go into some detail about marketing definitions and concepts. Care has been used to avoid esoteric terms and vocabulary. Practitioners will be familiar with all the marketing concepts and terminology used but a reminder is always useful for clarity and comprehension; the references on page 00 to books and other publications should prove of value to readers wanting further information and analysis.

## Perspectives

In the nineteenth century, charities such as Barnardo's appealed directly to the public's existing value systems. Advertisements were placed in newspapers such as *The Times* to appeal to the middle and upper classes who, it was hoped, possessed both the capacity and propensity to give to the less well off – especially when the cause was needy children.

By the 1920s and 1930s, by contrast, American for-profit advertisers had learned how consumers could be encouraged to identify with products and services as they discovered the role of sponsorship. The first soap operas were just that – continuing radio sagas of everyday life/loves/dramas paid for, through sponsorship, by washing powder and soap manufacturers. People's aspirations towards particular lifestyles were recognised by those marketeers and their advertising agencies and much of the scripting, whilst not yet making use of overt product placement, certainly gave rise to the linkages that advertisers today seek to create in their own scripts, graphics and story telling.

## Professional marketing

Once the power of advertising and public relations had been grasped – mainly by Fast Moving Consumer Goods (FMCG) manufacturers in the 1920s – it was only a question of time before the academics starting studying the subject and during the 1960s research into consumer behaviour became a recognised discipline.

In the UK, the Sales Managers Association was first formed in May 1911. In 1931 the name of this Association's magazine was changed to reflect the much wider subject area it covered – *Marketing*. It took until 1960, and much debate, to change the organisation's name to The Institute of Marketing and Sales Management. Finally in 1968 the name became simply the Institute of Marketing and in 1989 the institute was awarded its charter mark and is now the Chartered Institute of Marketing (CIM).

For not-for-profits seeking well qualified marketeers, the close similarity of service marketing to that of their own means that recruiters can look with confidence on membership of the CIM as demonstrating a well grounded understanding of their needs. The rigour of academic achievement should be matched with a pragmatic understanding born of experience.

## Linkage

The early work of Harold Sumption, George Smith and others (Allford 1993) built on their successful design of newspaper advertisement appeals; the use of simple typography and layout gave the impression of a rushed, cheaply-done job conveying 'urgent message requiring immediate response'. The technique was not confined to newspaper advertising; it was also used in direct mail, initially to existing supporters but soon to lists of targeted individuals who, it was thought, might share the same concerns and values of those who had already proven their interest.

Such work was crude by today's sophisticated targeting techniques. Attributes such as recency, frequency and monetary value (RFV|)

had yet to be identified as ways of segmenting donor lists, whilst predictors of likely behaviour and lifestyle lists hadn't been invented. Nevertheless the application of such marketing techniques worked wonderfully well and response rates in double figures to cold mailings were not unusual.

Practitioners such as Oxfam's Guy Stringer began to wonder if greater use could not be made of such successful practices, without compromising core values and integrity. In the face of trustee ignorance (if not actually hostility), however, few other charities at that time made much headway and only began to adopt, piecemeal, marketing practices that had been seen to work; these were rarely imbued with a corporate understanding of where such strategies would lead.

---

### COMMERCIAL CASE STUDY  HSBC

In the 1990s the Hong Kong and Shanghai Bank (HSBC), having recently acquired the Midland Bank in the UK, were also looking for growth and expanding sales, increasing market share and generating greater profitability.

This is a particularly useful example of an international organisation understanding and building upon existing reputations and beliefs. When the HSBC took over the Midland, one of the four major high street banks in the UK, many were very wary of the impact such a takeover would have. The Midland had several hundred thousand loyal (well at least long-term) customers who liked the philosophy captured in the friendly smiling Griffin (the Midland logo at that time) with the strapline, 'the listening bank'. Everything that HSBC has done has retained that basic belief and attitude. The griffin went and the red double triangle appeared. Then the name went and HSBC appeared with the double triangle. But core beliefs remained consistent. Advertising in the summer of 2002 still talks of HSBC as the local bank, implying that it is still there, listening and ready to act for you the customer.

---

# Not-for-profit branding

The British Rheumatism and Arthritis Association (BRA), which had been formed in 1947 by a remarkable young man named Arthur Mainwaring-Bowen, was perhaps the first not-for-profit to demonstrate some understanding of brand values. Waring (as he was known), had been diagnosed with Ankylosing Spondylitis (a particularly painful form of arthritis affecting the spine) and decided that, in the absence of useful user information for people with arthritis, he would form a lay organisation to help provide information and support.

By 1983 the organisation had grown very considerably, helping thousands of people with arthritis and employing a small but very active professional team aided by hundreds of volunteers, themselves often people with arthritis. However the name had become a hindrance to further expansion and understanding of the organisation's mission. Confusion around the medical terms and the actual work of the charity abounded because there was no clear indication of the organisation's work in its name. Indeed many thought it a professional association for rheumatologists. Despite misgivings and apprehension the trustees accepted the need and agreed to change the name to Arthritis Care. This, in the early 1980s, nicely espoused a punchy yet caring ethos which said, very simply, 'this is a charity that cares for people with arthritis and provides support for them'.

BRA never funded medical research. That activity was, unusually for medically orientated charities, the remit of a completely separate charity – The Arthritis and Rheumatism Council – which has now also changed its name to the Arthritis Research Campaign retaining its well known acronym (ARC). This change shows some understanding of the public's propensity to trust a name that it recognises. Arthritis and research are both words the general public will recognise and therefore assume that they have already heard of a charity called Arthritis Research: in the same way, most people believe there is a charity called, simply, Cancer Research (which CRUK has cleverly taken ownership of).

After the changes, Arthritis Care entered a decade of strong growth through a rapid expansion of its branch structure (all run by volunteers) and membership which peaked in the mid-1990s at more than 70,000. Whilst marketing had not necessarily been accepted as a complete function within the organisation, the practices involved in brand management and the need to foster understanding through effective PR had been successfully employed.

# Market research

In 1957 Ford in the USA introduced the first car ever to have been designed and brought to market using extensive market research. A huge programme of quantitative and qualitative research was conducted and analysed. From this designers took their brief to create a 'classic 1950s saloon car' with big tail fins, sculpted looks, high on luxury and endeavouring to provide a 'feel good factor' for both men (identified as the prime buyers) and women (seen as secondary decision influencers). The car was called the 'Edsell' after Henry Ford's son.

The car was launched amidst a barrage of advertising and press comment. Sadly, despite the intention to 'satisfy customer needs' (in this case to design and bring to market at the right price the car that a vast number of American families would buy and enjoy owning) it failed rather spectacularly.

One theory about its failure concerns the shortcomings of the market research. What researchers didn't include (and at the time perhaps could be forgiven for not considering) was a forward prediction as to the likes and dislikes of American society 12 months and two years after the car's launch. What happened? In 1958 the Russians launched Sputnik, the first man-made orbital satellite, and America realised it had lost that round of the space race. In turn the complacency that had characterised the late 1950s in the USA turned to a new era of, if not austerity, then certainly realism and a desire to regain the lead in world technology. Almost overnight tastes changed. Overt opulence was out, efficiency, more austere lines and modest fittings characterised the cars of the next decade. Tail fins were dead and the Edsell died with them.

Whatever the real reasons for the radical shift in American tastes and behaviour it showed that market research is only part of the picture. Marketeers were still learning.

# Marketing research

Another crucial aspect of research is not just what the market wants, or thinks it wants, but what is already being produced, that is the competition, the totality of the market and the relative market shares that each of the main players enjoy. From this an individual organisation can begin to identify its own internal Strengths and Weaknesses and external Opportunities and Threats. Usually known as a SWOT analysis this component is crucial in helping to identify in what direction any organisation, for-profit or not-for-profit , should be moving. The use of this and other analytic tools such as the PEST analysis (Political, Economic, Social and Technical factors) is examined in the next chapter.

---

**CASE STUDY LEONARD CHESHIRE**

Leonard Cheshire in 2000–01, when faced with huge potential changes in the market for care services for disabled people and, in particular, residential services for disabled people, conducted a wide ranging 12-month review of its activities and resources together with commissioned external research from Ashridge Management Centre. The review was in response to the government's introduction from April 2002 of new residential care standards that, for the first time ever, differentiated between the standards required for disabled people and the frail elderly. During the previous 40 years the charity had built up a huge range of residential services ranging from large rambling country houses to small state of the art supported living units where every resident had their own front door. Some 120 buildings were involved and for the first time the charity discovered that it was the market leader in providing residential care for disabled people. It also learned that, if it were to modernise all its residential places (and market indicators pointed towards an overall similar requirement for places over ten years though with increasing levels of support), it would need to invest up to £100 million over the next five years. As a result a complete strategic review of all the charity's operations was completed and a new strategic plan developed. A clear example of how marketing research can drive strategic planning.

# Marketing practices

Direct marketing is often thought of as direct mail but also includes the use of telephone, the Internet and now, interestingly, a return to face-to-face dialogue in the form of street, workplace and house-to-house canvassing. There is nothing new in all this, as brush salesmen were selling door-to-door in the early twentieth century. What is perhaps different is the use that charities in particular make of these practices, often excelling in their execution and getting response rates that are the envy of the commercial sector. When the Brooke Hospital for Animals began to ask their 20,000 loyal supporters for regular donations they enjoyed response rates in excess of 30 per cent. Similarly early cold mailings to carefully selected lists of those already interested in animal welfare returned better than 10 per cent.

Redmond Mullin (2002) comments that some of St Paul's letters are amongst the best fundraising letters ever written. Two thousand years on it perhaps indicates that there really is very little new under the sun. Nothing new perhaps, but, always there is always an opportunity to refine, find a new twist or use in an innovative way.

The enormous growth of direct dialogue canvassing – the use of paid fundraisers to ask people face-to-face in the street to sign a monthly direct debit there and then – has enabled many larger well known charities dramatically to increase their databases of regular donors. Moreover the profile of these new supporters tends to be far younger than that of traditional responders to direct mail. Profiling conducted in 2000 showed an average donor to be under 30 years of age. Concerns voiced by local authorities and some commentators that the technique was becoming too intrusive has led to the formation of the PFRA (Public Fundraising Regulatory Authority) with its first high profile chair, Tim Hornsby ex chief executive of the NLCB. They will have their work cut out to manage the process of self-regulation. Chapter nine analyses some of the possible consequences of the review of charity law by the cabinet of the strategy unit. However Caring Together, one of the largest agencies operating in this field, has developed an innovative solution to the question of overload.

---

CASE STUDY **CARING TOGETHER**

Working with a small number of National Charities in 1998 Caring Together developed an approach to canvassing using the system of licenses that charities have operated under for many years. This is the system of going literally house to house, doorstep to doorstep in the tradition of earlier travelling pedlars and the brush salesmen that followed them. Local Authorities grant licences for house-to-house collections which ensures that people in any particular area do not get three different collectors in the same week. Instead of the collecting tin or envelope, however, a canvasser will attempt to interest the householder or occupier in the idea of a tax efficient regular small donation to a favourite cause. Often those responding positively do so with an average donation of 33p per day or £10 per month. Since direct mail responders rarely give more than a single £20 donation, this practice is enormously cost effective. Cathy Sullivan, founder and chief executive of Caring Together, adds: 'Face-to-face fundraising is now maturing. Some say it has a limited lifetime and it will certainly begin to plateau in future years. However, reports of its demise are indeed premature as they fail to take into account several very important factors. The population of the United Kingdom continues to increase and new generations trade places ensuring there will always be a new potential audience for a cause. Furthermore, many people support more than one cause and do so in a variety of ways, because they've been motivated and asked. So just as direct mail and telephone fundraising have settled into being viewed as traditional, so will face-to-face.'

---

# The limits of marketing

It is sometimes helpful to define through negatives; marketing cannot provide all the answers. Too often organisations have turned to marketing to help them through difficult times. Poor product take-up is seen as a failure of advertising rather than necessarily of poor design, distribution or pricing. Marketing can help identify needs and ways to fulfil them but it isn't the complete picture, though many marketing directors might have you believe that it is. That should be the role of the organisation's overall strategy flowing from its core vision and mission. This is examined further in Chapter three.

Most marketing texts analyse the constituent elements of marketing into 'the four Ps', for example McDonald (1995). On the other hand Ian Bruce in his excellent book (1998) defines the usual terms – Product, Promotion, Price and Place – plus a fifth one Position. Further discussion of these definitions will be found in Chapter three of this book; for many readers not completely familiar with this analysis of the marketing mix it may therefore be worth a forward look. In reality marketing can be segmented into many more elements and so is not simply a matter of identifying the Ps, whether four, five or eight. An understanding of the totality and its effective application is what defines successful marketeers.

For example market research and marketing research are very important aspects of defining the market needs and an organisation's ability to meet them. Sometimes however all the research in the world cannot predict events.

# Conclusion

Good marketing people can always construct, add or design a new twist to old methds of fundraising. Face-to-face fundraising by canvassers, in the street is not, in itself, a new idea. Volunteers have been conducting collections for decades. The advent of the direct debit, so that supporters pledge, typically, £5 per month – Gift Aided – rather than put 50p or £1 in the collecting tin or envelope has, however, revolutionised the technique.

Crucially organisations have learned that they need to build their brand by investing across the marketing mix and across all audiences. That is they invest precious resources in each of the marketing elements such as promotion, pricing and positioning in addition to more basic questions of products, services, distribution and target market segments. Chapter three looks at this in greater detail. In order for there to be coherence in brand development, however, the most important single requirement is for an integrated marketing strategy to be developed, agreed and implemented. The next chapter considers all the necessary steps.

# Preparing a marketing strategy

'When you see the right cause, act; do not wait for
orders.'
*Sun Tzu*

'Good plans shape good decisions. That's why good planning
helps to make elusive dreams come true.'
*Lester Bittel*

Today, marketing is an acknowledged constituent of nearly all organisations, including even the smallest charities and one person businesses. However for many, especially within the not-for-profit sector, marketing is still very much regarded as an add-on, a luxury even, or perhaps as a function 'bolted on' alongside fundraising and communications rather than an integral part of an organisation's overall vision and mission.

A main argument of this book is that strategic marketing needs to be fully integrated into an entire organisation's plans and operations so that it becomes part of the culture. This chapter explains why a clear marketing strategy must come first. It outlines the essential elements of a strategy and shows how that strategy must be grounded in the organisation's own mission and strategic objectives.

## Integration

Given this need to ensure clarity and a concurrence of goals it seems unlikely that a stand-alone marketing strategy, however well planned and executed, will achieve all that it should towards enabling an organisation to fulfil its overall objectives.

It may be helpful to use the analogy of the American space programme. The *vision*, the crucial ultimate goal for going into space would be 'To reach the stars'. Following President Kennedy's challenge in 1961 in response to the Russian lead in the space race, NASA set itself the *mission* which was to get a manned spacecraft to the Moon (and safely back again) before the end of that decade.

The strategic plan was the progressive programme of Mercury, Gemini, and Apollo with eventually *Apollo 11* landing on the moon on 19 July 1969. Armstrong, Aldrin and Shepherd returned home safely a week later. Each part of the mission had specific objectives; achievable aims against which progress could be measured. The vision remains but that particular part of the mission was achieved successfully.

Redmond Mullin (2002) reminds us that 'strategy' is originally a military concept and illustrates the hierarchy of levels between planning and execution as illustrated in Figure 2:

**FIGURE 2** PLANNING PROCESS HIERARCHY

STRATEGIC → OPERATIONAL → TACTICAL

Dwight Eisenhower had something to say about the process: 'In preparing for battle I have always found that plans are useless, but planning is indispensable.' Mullin, quoting Clausewitz (1832) says, 'everything in strategy is very simple, but that does not mean it is very easy'.

# Differentiation

Marketing, if approached effectively, needs to permeate the entire management board and for that matter, the whole board of trustees or directors. Only when an organisation can embrace all the disciplines necessitated by a marketing-led approach will the benefits start to manifest themselves.

For example, marketing is essential to differentiate one charity from another, helping to identify and promote the unique proposition of any organisation. This might be simply that a charity operates in the north of England as opposed to another that only serves the Birmingham area, or that one organisation provides information to the public as opposed to another that campaigns for change by local or national government. On the other hand competing medical research charities may need to promote the unique aspects of their work.

Igor Ansoff (1918–2001) was one of the first academics to recognise the need for the concept of strategic management. In a published article, he simplified his concept into two sentences.

- 'The key to strategy is recognizing that if a company is functioning, it is part of the environment.'

- 'When a Manager understands the environment and recognizes that the environment is constantly changing, then the manager can make the correct decisions in leading the organisations into the future.'

Dr Ansoff (1968) theorised that if a company becomes purely self-serving, it soon loses track of its direction and dies. He believed that long-term profitability results from a commitment to understanding the political and social fabric of a community. This is an important consideration underlining the need to ensure that for-profits work together with not-for-profits to achieve these mutual objectives. It is an early indication that corporate social responsibility (CSR) should be an integral part of a company's strategy and not just a reaction to public opinion.

# The marketing plan

Logically many will start with the marketing plan. It is, as has been discussed, possible for the marketing imperatives to drive strategy. It is however far more usual that the strategic direction, if not a full strategic plan, will already be in existence before questions are asked as to how the funding and resources necessary to achieve the agreed objectives can be generated. Ideally this becomes an iterative process as shown in Figure 3.

**FIGURE 3** STRATEGIC PLANNING PROCESS

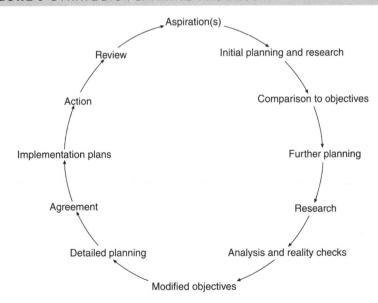

Aspiration(s)

Review

Initial planning and research

Action

Comparison to objectives

Implementation plans

Further planning

Agreement

Research

Detailed planning

Analysis and reality checks

Modified objectives

The reasons behind this iterative process are manifold. As David Saint, chair of Action Planning says (interviewed in 2002), 'the pressure to plan strategically often comes from fundraising who are expected to quantify their plans; charities often act intuitively – they are effective – but the direction isn't written down, so how can fundraisers be clear about their planning environment?' Saint goes on, 'open conversations with chief executives are crucial to establish a strategic planning framework, indeed without mentioning marketing the strategic plan can be the Trojan horse by which marketing can be introduced'.

Let us look first at marketing planning in more detail.

# Analysis and planning

The case of the Ford Edsell (p24–5) shows how wrong one can be to depend entirely upon market research. That said increasing numbers of charities are realising that specific appropriate research is a vital element in the development of any meaningful strategy. It is important that the need for particular research is properly understood so that the right questions are asked. In the same way the differences between market planning and marketing planning need to be fully understood.

- Market planning looks carefully at the market itself – overall size, competition, potential growth and segmentation.

- Marketing planning looks more deeply at demand, user practices and aspirations and the position that an organisation should adopt or seek to move to in order to meet its strategic objectives.

Thus the important distinction between market research and market*ing* research must also be grasped if the right questions are to be asked, and answered to everyone's satisfaction.

# The Five Ps

Within the marketing mix it is helpful to think of the different elements that make up an organisation's offering to its chosen audiences. This helps to analyse the areas into functional responsibilities and to gain ownership of the plans and intended actions at an early opportunity, when there is still time to make meaningful changes. Usually these are broken into 'the Four Ps' (Product, Price, Promotion and Place) but as will be seen a fifth (Position) should be considered as a vital part of the overall mix.

The following matrix, probably the best known work of Ansoff and first postulated in the 1960s, is particularly useful to bear in mind throughout the planning process in terms of current and future development:

**FIGURE 4** ANSOFF'S MATRIX

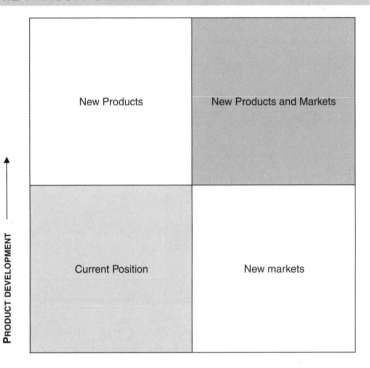

As shown in Figure 4 most organisations start in the bottom left hand corner, thinking about their current products and services that are supplied to current customers or users. Marketing planning usually concentrates on development towards new markets or new products or both. Clearly either route involves risk but the highest risk with the greatest danger of failure is to move towards new markets with new products or services. Equally it is true that with sufficient planning and resources the greatest success in terms of growth may arise from such a manoeuvre.

The matrix can be used in a number of different ways. As the basic model shows, when Leonard Cheshire applied the matrix to their services it looked as illustrated in Figure 4.1.

**FIGURE 4.1** LEONARD CHESHIRE'S APPLICATION OF ANSOFF'S MATRIX

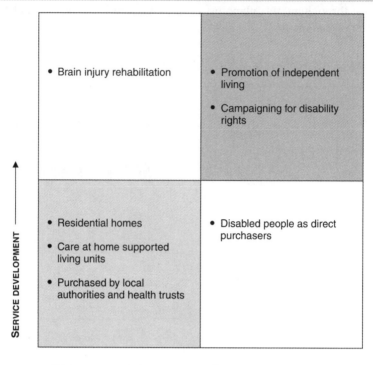

One of the major challenges for the organisation will be how to manage some of the transitions (especially in funding) that result as the mix of services begins to change over the next decade.

However the matrix can also be used to help understand the current (and possible future) of the fundraising product portfolio. With the example shown in Figure 4.2 service purchasers, as opposed to voluntary income providers, have been excluded and the range simplified to illustrate the analysis more clearly.

**FIGURE 4.2** LEONARD CHESHIRE'S FUNDRAISING APPLICATION OF ANSOFF'S MATRIX

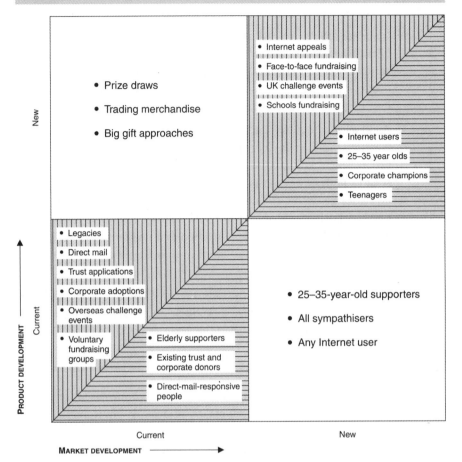

Thus legacies come from elderly supporters whilst face-to-face canvassing is aimed at 30-year-old sympathisers. Direct mail (DM) is currently sent to those responsive to this medium, whilst prize draws (UK-wide draws are a new venture for the charity) are targeted at supporters and all other sympathisers. Approaches to trusts and companies are reasonably self-explanatory though new approaches within target companies are aimed at persuading key decision makers and influencers to become or persuade others to become internal champions for the charity. Similarly the attempt to make Internet appeals work is aimed at specific groups within the total Internet user community. In the same way trading is a new venture for the charity which has not, historically, competed in the shop market or developed any coherent merchandising strategy. Both DM and Internet opportunities therefore exist and as the charity has overseas self-sufficiency projects it is investigating the ethical marketing of products sourced from such projects. These are however higher risk than the placing of new fundraising product to existing and new customers.

Overseas challenge events which, as for many charities, are in decline are being replaced by far more cost effective UK sponsorship events such as abseils and parachute jumps. Mass participation events such as the London marathon appeal to specific groups who, first and foremost, want to participate.

Another new activity for the organisation is specific approaches to wealthy individuals for major gifts. Income from UK voluntary groups such as Lions, Round Table and Rotary are static but the schools market has yet to be tapped. With the increasing emphasis on materials fitting the national curriculum there is an opportunity for the charity to develop and place suitable materials around disability equality issues, as an education and awareness vehicle. However this is a high risk investment in that the approach is for new products to new markets.

During the planning process one can go a step further with the analysis of existing fundraising products and chart them against the Boston Matrix as shown later in this chapter (p42).

## The Five Ps – product

The consideration and planning required to improve an organisation's core activity – its products or service – is often thought of as self-evident, but that is to confuse selling with marketing. Sales is essentially about getting today's products and services to those people who are willing to buy or, more usually with charities, to those who most need the services being offered. Marketing can be perceived as 'selling tomorrow's products'. This at least has the merit of allowing the question 'how should tomorrow's products and services be different' and by analogy 'should we be catering for different audiences?' In the planning process it is crucial to pose these questions. For fundraisers charged with this process it is vital to involve the operational part of the charity so that the main services of the organisation are considered as part of the marketing mix, not just the fundraising products and services. The results of external research should play an important part in the analysis, considering carefully what competitors and other organisations are offering and planning to offer. Equally market research can help to identify areas and audiences not served by existing offerings or requiring slightly different products/services to those currently on offer.

# The Five Ps – price

Very careful consideration of what is offered by competitors against comparative market share (or at least market position) is needed. For service-providing charities such as Leonard Cheshire, who contract with local authorities to provide care at home and residential services for disabled people, there are two distinct components:

- what the customer will pay (and in this case local authorities are notoriously price sensitive);

- what the competition is charging (and there always is competition – perhaps not always apparent).

Leonard Cheshire for example have built a very detailed pricing and costing model showing exactly what it costs to provide a week's residential care for any particular level of impairment. Frequently this is significantly higher than the price that local authorities have been willing to pay.

Through detailed negotiations, complete transparency and comparisons with valid like-for-like competition, the charity has been able to achieve very significant uplifts, albeit sometimes phased over two or three years, for the provision of existing care. It is important to note that this does not take into account compliance with the new care standards introduced in April 2002 which, in effect, require suppliers, not-for-profit and for-profit, to offer a new product. That is, a level of residential care to specific detailed criteria such as room sizes and levels of staffing that were not formerly recognised.

In consumer markets it is vital to understand the 'elasticity of demand'. (Thirkettle 1970 *et al.*). Within many inelastic markets, because competition is so fierce small increases in price, say, for cornflakes may lead to significant shifts in demand as consumers switch their buying patterns, even away from the market leader. In other elastic markets a price rise may have little effect on demand. Interestingly this can be seen in the humble charity shop or on the bookstall in the jumble sale where the author altered the price of second-hand paperbacks on sale from 20p each to 40p each. The result was that demand changed not at all whilst monetary turnover doubled. Buyers either wanted a particular title or not, and having found it were certainly prepared to spend 40p on acquiring it. An interesting experiment, at subsequent sales, might have been to go on raising the price until demand began to fall and then revert to the one delivering maximum returns.

# The Five Ps – promotion

Many see this simply as the provenance of advertising but this part of the marketing mix goes so much further. Branding and the building of brand values is achieved largely through the use of an effective communication programme, having first ensured that the product is right. Promotion covers all aspects of advertising, use of media and media coverage, public relations, internal and external communications, customer/client relations, after sales service and much more. An integrated plan is required which ensures that all channels through which news and information can reach customers and users are addressed, and that a suitable programme is built and delivered to meet the required level of exposure.

'Orange' is a particularly good commercial example of a complete brand being built, principally through advertising. Early advertisements showed no product, merely a concept, 'the future's bright, the future's orange'. In just six words the advertisers were able to propose an optimistic statement with which most would want to agree and then use repetition to inculcate the brand name – a colour and a fruit liked by the vast majority of the population. Much editorial comment followed and by the time the actual product started appearing everyone was familiar with, and generally well disposed towards, the brand and the values espoused. Promotion continues through the whole communications process – sales incentives and display activities all the way to customer care and after sales service – to ensure that the messages stay consistent and users remain satisfied with their investment. This was an excellent piece of marketing in that access to cellular technology had, in effect, become a commodity where, usually, price is king.

## CASE STUDY  NSPCC

The NSPCC also used the full range of promotional tools in building and launching the 'Full Stop' campaign. For a charity to commit itself very publicly to ending child cruelty was a brave (and some might say foolhardy) thing to do. Yet in reality it is only a restatement of the organisation's vision and mission: a clear, unequivocal, public restatement but a big bold idea that does capture the imagination. The advertising and communications programme that followed the launch succeeded in reaching many people previously sympathetic to the charity but sufficiently unmoved to have actively supported them. And whilst the appeal target of £250 million may not have been achieved within the stated timeframes the NSPCC itself remains convinced that it was the right campaign at the right time. As Giles Pegram, the organisation's long-time director of appeals, said at the International Fundraising Congress (October 2002), the charity has raised £110 million of new money and continues with its strategy to raise £250 million. The campaign also links rather neatly into the government's own commitment to end child poverty, one of the major causes of child abuse.

## The Five Ps - place

This covers the whole subject more properly defined as distribution. That is, how and where customer needs are met. For example with a Leonard Cheshire residential care home this may well be seen as a given, yet one that needs to change. Historically many homes were sited where a convenient property existed, an old country house willed to the charity or, in the case of Staunton Harold (situated in Derbyshire), rescued from demolition by dint of a government grant and direct pressure on the family owners. Unfortunately such locations, though set in beautiful parks in rolling countryside, are no longer acceptable to the majority of people who, increasingly, would rather have their own front doors and easy access to community facilities such as shops, pubs and cinemas. The Care Standards Act enshrines this need for disabled people and the charity has embarked upon an extensive modernisation/new build programme.

Distribution for the retail industry is a science in its own right. Logistics covers the whole gamut of the supply of the right goods into the right outlets in the right quantities at the right time. Supermarkets depend upon 'just in time' systems. Fundraisers charged with delivering income growth through trading subsidiaries and shop chains are learning the same skills in order to improve profitability and customer satisfaction.

Place is an important part of the marketing mix sometimes overlooked when the provision of services – such as information – is again taken for granted via existing channels such as information leaflets and helplines. However as the enormous take-up and growth in Internet services has shown change is always with us and is perhaps the only constant that should be factored into marketing plans. How an organisation delivers its services is as important as the physical 'where', and both can be contained within considerations of distribution.

## The Five Ps - position

The preceding elements, product, price, promotion and place are usually considered in depth within the analysis for a marketing plan. However it is helpful to think of positioning both in terms of individual products and the organisation itself in any strategic plan.

Not only does an organisation need to consider on what basis it will compete within a chosen segment or marketing (for example high priced, low volume Rolls Royce or low priced, high volume Ford Ka) but often as an organisation a strategic positioning response is called for in terms of an organisation's core mission and objectives. (For example the NSPCC, in seeking to end child cruelty, has to be seen as credible, authoritative and very well resourced because such an outcome will take a huge investment to achieve.)

Ries and Trout (1981) claim that when considering the issue of position organisations have three distinct alternatives to pursue. First, an organisation can build upon its current position to create a distinctive perception of the brand by customers and target audiences. Avis consistently used the 'we try harder' to make a virtue out of being number two to Hertz in the car hire market. Second, having established the attributes that are most important to its chosen audiences, users, customers or supporters, the organisation can see if there are any unoccupied positions that are desirable in the audience's minds and therefore viable opportunities or positions to take up. Drummond and Ensor (2001) quote the example of IDV Ltd who looked at traditional sweet dark sherries versus pale and light dry sherries and identified an opportunity for a light coloured sweet sherry. They launched Croft Original at a time when there was no other competitor and it is now the best selling sherry brand in the UK.

The third option open to organisations is where there has been a change in consumer behaviour, in society's attitudes or perhaps even an error in the original position adopted. At this point repositioning may be considered. Many companies and charities attempt to reposition themselves in response to changing circumstances or market developments but this is not an easy task to perform successfully. Babycham abandoned the famous deer and trademark green bottle in 1993 in an effort to appeal to a wider market including young men. However by 1997 it had abandoned all the changes, reverting to the traditional marks and returning to an appeal to a predominantly female audience. Charities are currently investing a great deal in name changes and recent examples include: British Diabetic Association to Diabetes UK; Marriage Guidance Council to Relate; The Distressed Gentlefolk's Association to Elizabeth Finn Trust; The Sue Ryder Foundation to Ryder Care, amongst many others. These changes were made partly in response to a perceived need to reposition themselves and to appeal to larger audiences. Where there is a very clear need to reposition the investment necessitated by a name and logo change may be justified, but in many cases changes are made for the sake of doing something different.

Interestingly repositioning can work very effectively for fundraising products. Many charities are experiencing over-capacity and declining demand for overseas challenge events and the Brooke Hospital for Animals is no exception. However in their case, anyone visiting a Brooke project offering free veterinary care to working horses, mules and donkeys in Egypt, Jordan, India, Pakistan and Afghanistan tends to become a very loyal, long-term supporter and advocate of the charity. By moving visits away from the challenge element and concentrating on the paid visit by supporters and their friends a significant boost to the high value donor programme has been engineered.

Stephen Pidgeon, chairman of the direct marketing agency Target Direct, has closely observed the efforts and detailed analysis of some not-for-profits attempts to define or redefine their position. He thinks there are some good examples of organisations simply aiming to clarify what they are about. For example he cites the National Trust in Scotland who have built upon the very Scottishness of the organisation – 'the heart of the nation' – and clearly incorporated that idea into their fundraising propositions, hoping for an organic growth in uptake and responses. He also points to the Salvation Army who have, in a similar way, consistently revisited their total, unjudgemental love of humanity and reflected that in their fundraising and communications messages – interestingly without any overt reference to their deep Christian beliefs that love of humanity is a reflection of godly love. Pidgeon feels that it is all too easy to change, with the best of intentions and get it wrong. For example, the DGFA change to Elizabeth Finn Trust (the name of their founder) has been done with the best intentions but does anyone recognise that name and, most importantly, will anyone equate that to an organisation working very hard on behalf of older people?

# Trustee and board ownership

Much of the impetus for 'vision' and 'mission' should be coming from the trustee board or board of directors, though as we saw from the Leonard Cheshire case study in the last chapter the pressure to review and change may well be marketing driven.

However derived, ownership of the strategy to enable effective marketing planning is crucial. The section on internal communications and the internal market later in this chapter (p52) talks about the communications necessary but before that stage it is vital to ensure ownership not just of the overall corporate objectives but specifically of the marketing strategy and objectives.

The process necessary to involve, gain understanding and ensure ownership from a board will require careful consideration of the individuals involved. Understanding and acceptance by the senior management team is a crucial part of the necessary plan. This at least will ensure that criticism or unhelpful counter tactics from, say, financial- or service-orientated board members can be identified and resolved long before they become an issue. One of the many useful analytical tools that may be used during planning is the Boston Matrix and the many variations that now exist. It is particularly helpful to generalist trustees or non-executive directors who are attempting to gain an insight into the processes involved, and the need to move in a particular direction; it can be adapted for use by just about any organisation, public, private or not-for-profit.

# The Boston Matrix

Whilst this is probably one of the best known models for portfolio analysis it is also one of the least understood and some expansion is appropriate here. Developed by the Boston Consulting Group, the standard matrix is concerned with the generation and use of cash within a business and can be used very effectively to analyse either a complete operation or business unit, or specific products and services. The two axes on the model represent relative market share and market growth. Relative market share is seen as a predictor of the ability to generate cash. This is based on the proposition that high market share translates into a high volume of sales whilst investment in marketing and maintaining that position will be relatively smaller, if only through economies of scale. On the other hand the potential for market growth is seen as a predictor of the need for cash investment in a product or service. Products in high growth sectors require proportionately far higher investment to keep up with demand and the competition. Figure 5 illustrates the matrix.

**FIGURE 5** AN ADAPTATION OF THE BOSTON MATRIX

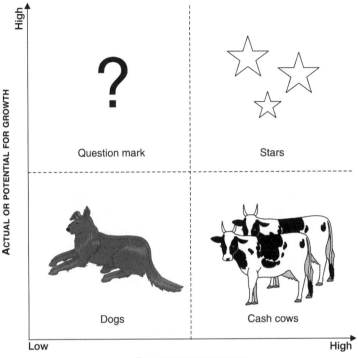

- 'Cash cows' is the term used for products enjoying a high market share in a relatively stable, mature market – thus they generate a positive cash flow.

- 'Stars' refer to, perhaps, newer products enjoying a high profile in an expanding market. Investment necessary to maintain the position is high and therefore cash flow may be neutral or less positive.

- 'Question marks' describe products in that sector where market share is low but the potential for growth remains high. Investment also therefore remains high and cash flow may well be negative.

- 'Dogs' (or even dead dogs) are seen as underperforming products in stable or declining markets with low or no growth and low relative market share. Cash flow is likely to be neutral or negative.

The great value of this analysis, when used accurately with appropriate research, is that decisions can be made about products or services within the portfolio.

- Should Question marks have further investment pumped in to turn them into Stars or should investment be cut right back to allow them either to die away or become a small Cash cow, perhaps occupying a particular niche market?

- As growth falls and markets mature should investment in Stars be frozen or cut back to 'milk' them as Cash cows?

- Should Dogs be put down, replaced, or updated and relaunched as a niche product?

The matrix is predicated upon the parallel concept, also devised by the Boston Consulting Group, of product lifecycles that is similarly one of the most quoted but possibly least understood concepts in marketing. The basic concept relates to four principal stages in the life of any product or service:

- introduction, when investment is high;

- growth, where investment continues and is even increased to ensure a high relative market share;

- maturity, when the market stabilises and investment may be cut back, and finally;

- decline, when sales fall and decisions need to be made about an individual product's future.

These can be mapped against the four segments of the matrix to crosscheck a product's actual position. It is of course vital to realise that an individual lifecycle may last a season (as in fashion clothing), some years (as with cars) or even decades (as with many food and drink brands). Reinvestment, product or service innovation and repositioning can of course put an existing product into an entirely new cycle.

For fundraisers the axes can be changed to reflect more helpful determinators so as to plot the effectiveness of individual fundraising propositions and products. For example if market share is replaced with 'resourcing need' or 'return on investment', and absolute market growth with a realistic assessment of the potential for growth, an individual not-for-profit organisation might plot its portfolio as shown in Figure 5.1.

**FIGURE 5.1** FUNDRAISING ADAPTATION OF THE BOSTON MATRIX

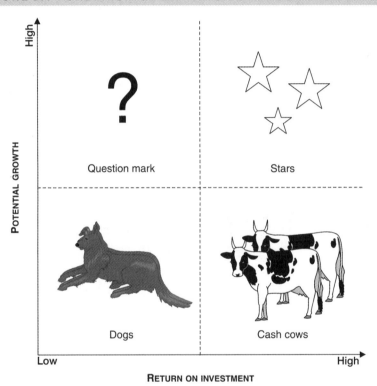

A further refinement may be to place each product within a circle denoting its relative contribution to the overall income. A simplified version for the Brooke Hospital for Animals might look like the illustration in Figure 5.2.

**FIGURE 5.2** BROOKE HOSPITAL FOR ANIMALS FUNDRAISING USE OF THE BOSTON MATRIX

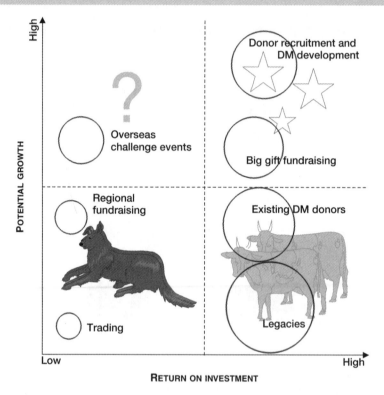

The matrix is highly adaptable to the individual needs of an organisation or sector as the following example shows. This has been adapted from Montanari and Bracker by Drummond and Ensor (2001) and Figure 5.3 shows how a public sector portfolio can be drawn up by a campaigning charity.

**FIGURE 5.3** A CAMPAIGNING APPLICATION OF THE BOSTON MATRIX

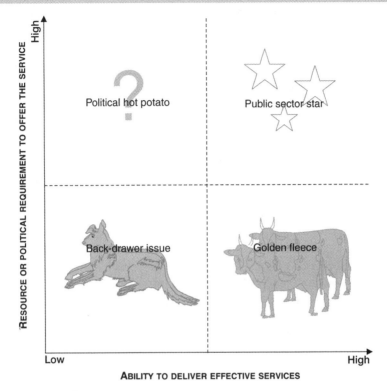

**ABILITY TO DELIVER EFFECTIVE SERVICES**

From this it should be possible to understand how issues could be mapped against the matrix to determine how best to apply scarce resources and effort.

Here the ability to deliver an effective campaign is mapped against the resources required to produce the desired results. Thus a low effort requirement coupled to a high ability to deliver on a particular issue creates a 'golden fleece' (from the myth of 'Jason and the argonauts'). Conversely, with a low ability to deliver and a high resource requirement, another issue becomes a 'political hot potato'.

# Competition

It would be wholly wrong to suggest that competition to charities can come only from other fundraising and voluntary organisations. A large number of charities are involved in the delivery of direct services to disabled people, those with terminal illnesses, animals, and other groups. Many of these services are delivered under contract with local social services departments, and there are many other not-for-profit and for-profit organisations delivering similar services and competing for the same contracts in many areas of the UK. Thus market research must look at the entirety of a given market – however imprecise the definitions – so that realistic projections and planning criteria can be adopted.

Only by conducting rigorous market research did Leonard Cheshire, doing a strategic review during 2000–01 discover that not only was it a major player in the provision of residential accommodation for disabled people (which it knew) but that it was in fact the market leader with more than 50 per cent of the total market. This significantly influenced the organisation's analysis and resulting strategy.

More usually not-for-profits occupy tiny niches within much larger market segments and often feel that such research is neither appropriate nor worthwhile since market leadership is not their objective. However a comprehensive review of every player in a chosen market or segment can be most revealing and offer opportunities for change, growth, amalgamation or partnership that would not otherwise have been envisaged. It is vital to have a clear understanding of who else is operating in the same areas, with similar or differing services, solutions or approaches. The same rigour that is taken as read in most commercial marketing departments should be applied to the planning process within not-for-profit organisations.

# Market audit

Before deciding upon new or revised objectives it is crucial to understand where the organisation is, not just in terms of the total market and its competition, but also internally: how is it performing against existing plans, objectives or simple aspirations? A SWOT analysis (as shown in Figure 6), looking inwardly at the organisation's strengths and weaknesses and externally at opportunities and threats is a useful way of examining the situation.

**FIGURE 6** THE SWOT ANALYSIS

| | |
|---|---|
| STRENGTHS | WEAKNESSES |
| OPPORTUNITIES | THREATS |

This always helps to focus the mind and determine many of the ingredients of the marketing mix. By charting the organisation's strengths and weaknesses (usually the internal view) and contrasting them with the opportunities and threats (generally external) it becomes clear where progress needs to be made and often indicates, in terms of marketing development, where it should be looking in terms of the Ansoff matrix illustrated in Figure 4, p33. This process will help to determine, amongst other things, whether new services or new audiences should indeed be the highest priority. Having done this for the organisation as a whole, fundraisers may find it helpful to conduct a SWOT analysis purely for the fundraising activities. This should show up any particular incongruencies or, just as important, areas of synergy between the organisation's core activities and its fundraising programmes.

CASE STUDY **BROOKE HOSPITAL FOR ANIMALS**

The Brooke Hospital for Animals had experienced a gradual increase in voluntary income through the late 1980s and early 1990s as a result of the activities of highly motivated volunteers and (perhaps as a result) substantial growth in legacy income. Nevertheless expansion in its overseas work of providing free veterinary care for working horses, donkeys and mules resulted in an even more rapid growth in expenditure.

As a result annual deficits rose to a peak of £2.4 million in 1999–2000. A new chief executive was appointed and a fundraising audit commissioned. The SWOT analysis of the existing fundraising operation was as shown in Figure 6.1.

**FIGURE 6.1** BROOKE HOSPITAL FOR ANIMALS USE OF A SWOT ANALYSIS

| STRENGTHS | WEAKNESSES |
|---|---|
| • Passionate/loyal supporter database | • Very low public awareness |
| | • No fundraising structure |
| • Significant numbers of unprompted high-value donations | • Very little trust and corporate support |
| • Highly motivated local volunteers | • Over-dependency on legacy income |
| **OPPORTUNITIES** | **THREATS** |
| • Overseas aid work presents great case studies and photos | • Perception of limited scope |
| | • Reduced support by key donors |
| • Huge groundswell of middle England support for animal welfare | • Increased competition by larger players |
| • Existing supporters give unprompted | |

A similar tool, which is particularly useful for examining the external environment in rather more detail, is the PEST analysis as shown below in Figure 7.

Such an analysis enables an organisation to examine factors in its external environment that are likely to exert an influence. These factors are categorised into four areas – political, economic, social (or society) and technical (or technology).

**FIGURE 7** A PEST ANALYSIS

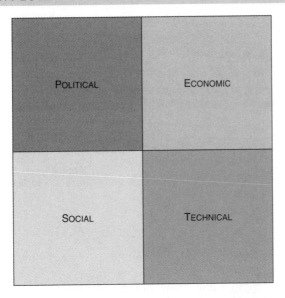

This is another valuable tool to assist boards, management groups and staff teams to examine the external factors likely to impact an organisation over any particular timeframe. For example a marketing group may attempt to look three years forward and forecast the factors that may impact their plans and therefore help to develop strategies to meet those changes and pressures.

## The use of research

Similarly, existing market research can be factored in to the analysis, or conversely the need to know much more about certain aspects of key markets or audiences may underline the requirement to conduct research qualitative or quantitative.

Given a clear understanding of the organisation's position relative to the total market, its competitors and organisations offering similar activities, it is then possible to begin drawing up a marketing plan detailing the objectives and the actions to be taken to achieve them. Figure 8 illustrates this process.

**FIGURE 8** A MARKETING PLANNING CYCLE

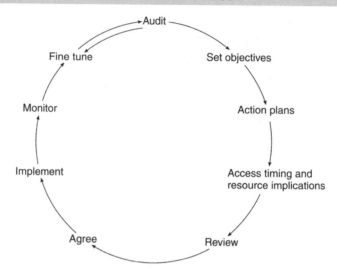

The marketing plan restates the organisation's objectives, as they relate to the marketing function, and provides a detailed set of agreed action plans to achieve those key targets. Once understood this process can indeed, in outline, be put together perhaps in an hour. However for greatest impact it is vital to obtain agreement and thence ownership from the board and every other department which has any influence at all upon the organisation's effectiveness.

# Internal communications

As the whole of this chapter postulates, developing a marketing plan needs to be part of a fully integrated process understood and agreed by the board and owned by the whole organisation. The most important audience for any marketeer is, in the view of Colin Mitchell (2002), the internal one. Mitchell asks, 'you tell your customers what makes you great but do your employees know?' He explains that internal marketing is so important because it is the best way to help employees (and by extension volunteers) to make a powerful emotional connection to the products and services that an organisation delivers. His view is that companies often ignore this fact and he continues: 'Employees are unified and inspired by a common sense of purpose and identity. Unfortunately, in most companies internal marketing is done poorly, if at all.' Mitchell argues fervently to link internal and external marketing so that staff understand and reinforce the messages that an organisation is trying to communicate to its chosen audience. Otherwise dissonance will interfere with otherwise powerfully-orchestrated implementation plans and campaigns. When a beleaguered British Rail prematurely launched a campaign announcing service improvements under the title of 'we're getting there' they provoked extremely destructive press comment by drawing attention to the void between the promise and reality. As a result, staff who had been quite legitimately proud of real progress that had been made were thoroughly demoralised. Mitchell advocates a five-step approach to the creation of an internal communications strategy that will engage staff. The same approach may be valuable in gaining internal acceptance, understanding and assistance to implement a new marketing plan.

- Don't preach – marketeers must draw on employee research to identify what staff are really thinking about, and ask rank and file staff articulate the hopes aspirations and vision.

- Emphasise beliefs – intentions are necessary but beliefs inspire and motivate people to care about the goals; intentions may change over time, the core beliefs should not.

- Make the medium part of the message – capture the attention and interest of the internal audiences by using surprise and intrigue, don't send out the same old memos and presentations; take risks and engage the audience.

- Design materials to fit – long tomes and manuals simply do not get read; IBM sent out a pamphlet along the lines of Chairman Mao's little red book, explaining why Linux was so important to the company's future, which was valued and actively used.

- Have fun – a cardinal rule for fundraising, it applies just as much to internal communications that can be self-important and boring; humour, self-deprecation and genuine humility can achieve remarkable results in communicating a message and gaining its acceptance.

# Sixty-minute plans

A strategic approach to the whole process takes a lot of time and needs to involve a very wide range of participants. Nevertheless a start has to be made somewhere and expectations laid upon an incoming new marketing executive can be very high. In addition much of the necessary work may already exist, albeit not in the form, detail and context required. Thus it is possible to draft a marketing plan fairly quickly if very clear, achievable corporate objectives already exist. That part is crucial. If the required information and clarity exists, the process (see Figure 9) might then look something like this:

**FIGURE 9** A SHORTENED MARKETING PLANNING PROCESS

Whilst far from ideal, the rigour of this shortened process – and the need to communicate at every stage – will initiate a journey during the course of which the organisation will come to understand what marketing, properly integrated and used, can achieve. It is highly likely in any existing organisation that plans and budgets exist. The reality checks that the process imposes however can be a very powerful aid to change and allow scope for far more detailed analysis and communication to proceed through to the next planning cycle. In the meantime the sixty-minute plan may be far more robust than targets and budgets 'plucked out of the chief executive's or chair's aspirations' or, more usually for fundraisers, last year's results plus 5 or 10 per cent.

# Comparisons

With the implementation of an effective marketing plan, charities can both raise awareness of the issues and enhance their position with chosen audiences. In order to be effective, the plan has to be grounded in thorough quantitative and qualitative research.

**FIGURE 10** CHART SHOWING CHARITIES' MARKET RESEARCH SPEND AS A PERCENTAGE OF TOTAL VOLUNTARY INCOME: 24 CHARITIES RESPONDED WITH INCOMES RANGING FROM £10 TO £100 MILLION PLUS (CROSSBOW 2002)

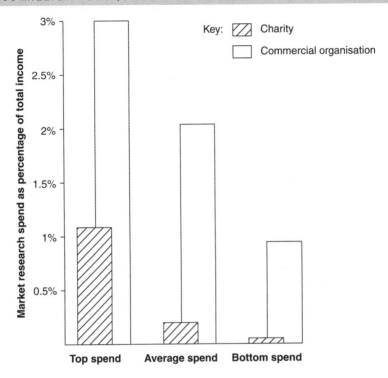

As one can see from the analysis in Figure 10, charities historically spend little on market research compared to many medium to large commercial organisations (who spend anything from 1 to 3 per cent of turnover on market research). But charities are learning. With the production of a meaningful, integrated marketing plan they are far more likely to generate the resources and power to achieve their stated strategic objectives. Once produced, a marketing plan should feed directly into the budgeting process so that there is an automatic review process, and updating on a quarterly, six monthly or annual basis becomes a normal part of the marketing activities. This iterative cycle is important in ensuring that plans do not get neatly bound and left on bookshelves.

# Conclusion

In brief then, whilst it is possible to outline plan in an hour it is far more important to ensure understanding and ownership of the plans by the entire organisation. Integration starts with the board but needs to work top down and bottom up. It is probably the most important element of any comprehensive plan and its role in helping ensure successful implementation cannot be overstated.

Objectives do need to be SMART. This to make them:

- specific – for clarity;

- measurable – to allow effective monitoring;

- aspirational – high enough to challenge and inspire high effort;

- realistic – targets must be achievable, and;

- timescaled with agreed milestones – to permit proper review and feedback.

However a variation of the normal criteria might allow for greater creativity and ownership and it is important not to become too mechanistic. Many of the objectives and measures should be non-financial and relate to the performance of the organisation as a whole. Non-profit organisations in particular need to consider outcomes rather than outputs. That is, the impact their work has rather than the way they spend their money. Most of all everything must contribute to the brand ensuring coherence in preserving and building upon the reputation of the organisation, as will be seen in the next chapter.

# CHAPTER FOUR

# The charity as a brand

'When I have finished, if a solution is not beautiful, I know it
is wrong.'                                                    *Buckminster-Fuller*

'I cannot and will not cut my conscience to fit this year's
fashions.'                                                    *Lillian Hellman*

Looking briefly at the origins and development of branding as a key element of the
marketing mix this chapter examines issues around brand values and how not-for-
profits in particular use their reputations to promote the objectives and work of the
organisation. Comparisons with commercial brands are made and key developments
examined for indicators of success. Some useful examples of rebranding exercises are
also examined and conclusions drawn.

# Perspectives

Branding was originally about ownership. Ancient Egyptian brick-
makers made a unique impression in the bricks they produced in
order to identify their own bricks, and thus the quantity they had
supplied to a site. Even human beings, over thousands of years of
slave trading, have been branded as someone's property; sadly this
practice still survives in some places today.

In the USA pioneer cattle ranchers literally branded their animals
by burning a unique mark, usually signifying the ranch name, into
the hides of their cattle. This was done in order to identify them
anywhere on the vast tracts of open range where they grazed, to
deter casual rustlers and make it easier to distinguish them at market. Farm animals and horses continue to be marked with a similar
security brand today.

The idea of an ownership mark signifying 'quality' or other distinct
values came to the fore with the advent of advertising, when manufacturers started putting their name on their products to establish a

competitive advantage over the offerings of others. At this point branding moved on from simply signifying ownership and began to represent the values and the qualities espoused by owners and manufacturers. This happened as the need to utilise improved production capacity and a reliable nationwide distribution network led manufacturers like Cadbury and Dunlop to adopt mass advertising techniques. Cadbury realised that he needed to stimulate demand for his products and began to promote values including 'goodness' and 'wholesomeness' to differentiate his chocolate from that of his competitors: the brand, as we know it, was born.

In 1870, Dr Thomas John Barnardo opened his first home for children in London's impoverished East End. He had been moved by the plight of large numbers of homeless children sleeping rough. Following the death of one boy who was turned away because the home was already over full, Barnado vowed 'never again'. His own name was used for the charity and he developed a strapline intended to make the values his charity espoused attention-grabbing: 'no child will ever be refused admission'. These words were painted in six-foot high letters over the gate of the home. Chapter 8 shows how Barnardo's today associates itself with attention-grabbing images of suffering, designed to be impossible to ignore.

# Brand identity

WWF has spent many years developing its corporate identity in order to clarify and emphasise the role of the organisation in environmental concerns, rather than in preserving threatened wildlife. As part of this new identity, it changed its name from the World Wildlife Fund to the World-wide Fund for Nature, whilst continuing to promote the well known WWF logo with its instantly recognisable Panda symbol. As Margaret Bennett (ex director of fundraising at WWF) says: 'There was great debate about the changes and some countries still have not fallen into line.' Despite that the WWF brand name and panda trademark is worth a great deal. Commercial marketeers know this and are prepared to pay for their brands to be linked to the panda. Interestingly WWF has vigorously defended the acronym successfully against the former World Wrestling Federation who have been forced to change their trading name to World Wrestling Enterprise.

The global brand IBM had to reinvent itself in the personal computer market after losing out badly to software rival Microsoft (Rodgers 1986). International Business Machines, the world leader in mainframe computers in the 1970s, soon became an also ran in the

PC market of the 1980s, when the DOS operating system was licensed by Microsoft to dozens of other manufacturers. Dell and Compaq, amongst others, sold far more PCs than IBM, who have subsequently revisited their roots and branded themselves as *the* company to provide a complete answer to networking, systems and E-commerce. With this approach, they are enjoying something of resurgence including the acquisition of PWC's consulting arm.

Leonard Cheshire, like Barnardo's another charity bearing its founder's name, has for some time been endeavouring to re-establish its brand. The charity is the UK's largest not-for-profit working with disabled people yet today has a prompted awareness of under 50 per cent of the adult population. From the 1960s to the 1980s the Leonard Cheshire Foundation benefited enormously from Cheshire's own celebrity status as a highly decorated Second World War hero and flying ace. Cheshire would write full page emotive articles in the national press, appear on television, radio and cinema and open new homes, often visiting exotic far away places. He was a charismatic figure and had a widespread public appeal. The charity attracted gifts, both large and small, from admirers who had been touched by his words and work.

Yet following Cheshire's death in 1992, the charity quickly realised that it had not built upon that celebrity status to establish a brand that could survive without its founder. There was no database of donors and knowledge of wealthy friends and favourably disposed trusts were at best in people's heads and at worst died with Cheshire. In 2001, while 80 per cent of men over 60 could recognise the charity's name, awareness among the under-35s had dropped to less than 20 per cent.

Adopting the disabled parking orange badge for its 'Enabled' campaign, Leonard Cheshire brought greater awareness to the issues of disability, but little to link this to its own master brand, to the extent that few people realised that Enabled was owned by the charity. The presentation of the brand was too fragmented. Later advertising sought to address this issue and reconnect the sub-brand of Enabled as an important part of Leonard Cheshire's work, with advertising targeted at younger age groups to strengthen this refocus. Consequently, all above and below the line marketing reflected the same issues, images and messages of 'enabling ordinary lives'.

The charity set up after the death of Diana Spencer made its own branding mistakes. The Memorial Fund was set up after Princess Diana's death in 1997. In the wake of the enormous surge of public sympathy, the fund was able to gain 'ownership' of the Diana brand, adopting the Princess's signature as its logo. However, some of its early decisions on how to market the brand, particularly allowing Flora margarine to feature the signature logo due to an association with the London Marathon, met with public and media criticism. More prudent decisions have been made since, and in its first three years the Fund made £35 million of grants with £100 million of assets. But, like many endowment funds it risks, in time, a gradual decline from public view as a new generation who never knew Diana replaces the one so deeply moved. It will be interesting to see how the Fund plans (if indeed it does) to refresh the brand in the future.

Even for a cause well known to the British public, branding work is seen as necessary. The Samaritans is rebranding for the first time in its 50-year history, in a bid to increase donations and boost volunteer numbers. Research for the charity found that while 90 per cent of the public is aware of its existence, few can accurately describe its services. Many of those surveyed said the charity simply supported people when they were suicidal. However, the organisation says it provides support to people across the emotional spectrum – not only those who are suicidal – and is therefore attempting to 'reposition' itself to improve public understanding of its role.

The Samaritans' volunteers, who are the key service deliverers, are being briefed about the rebranding, which has been developed by consultancy Wolff Olins and includes amending the charity's name to, simply, 'Samaritans'. A poster and press campaign will follow.

Simon Armson, the charity's chief executive, says there is a perception that people's problems have to be extreme before they contact a Samaritan. 'We're making it clear that suicide reduction remains very central to our philosophy, but that people may not be actively suicidal to need help and support,' he says. 'Samaritans is to do with coping and finding a way forward. That's what we've always been.' The rebranding also aims to expand the organisation's donor base. Armson continues: 'I hope that more people will want to donate to us and see that we are relevant. If they can see the organisation more clearly in its context, then hopefully it will be more attractive to them.'

# Unpacking brand identity

One helpful way of looking at this brand identity is to examine the 'three Ps of branding'; that is Personality, Physique, Presentation. It is useful when developing or implementing a brand strategy to analyse how the brand itself is perceived, in terms of its personality and physical attributes, and then how it is observed through its presentation in all guises. Figure 11 illustrates the relationships. Any dissonance will reflect badly upon the brand, creating confusion amongst potential customers and dissatisfaction amongst users.

**FIGURE 11** ELEMENTS OF BRAND IDENTITY

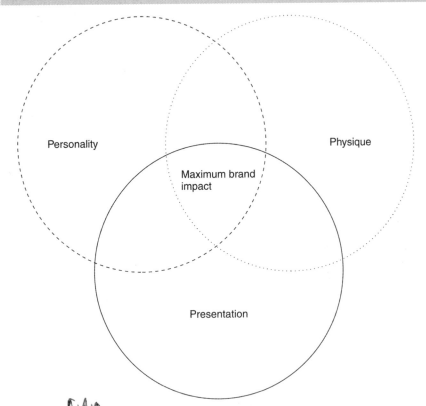

Brand personality (the very essence and soul of the proposition) should reflect the qualities and values espoused. In this way, Nike has used Michael Jordan to endorse and reflect the brand's youthful, virile, athletic, challenging and successful portrayal of life (as long as you wear the right trainers). It will be very important for the Diana Memorial Fund, as for any charity with a strong founder's image, to preserve at all costs the princess's personality in the ways that the Fund presents itself. Similarly the use of celebrity endorsement by charities must, crucially, fit with the organisation's existing values whilst avoiding conflict with planned programmes and possible changes. Only then can the not-for-profit seek meaningful sponsorship with corporates: these must be a good match with the celebrity's own persona, and offer a convincing fit between their commercial brand's values and those of the not-for-profit. Where such suitable corporate partners are found, a strong match has been established and a long-lasting, mutually beneficial relationship should result.

Brand physique (sometimes referred to as the tone of voice or the very feel of the offering) embraces the physical attributes of a product or organisation. For example, the United Colours of Benetton has chosen to portray itself as aggressive and challenging in its above the line advertising. Many of the images used by Benetton are certainly shocking, but whether this is, in the long term, successful in helping to sell expensive clothing remains to be seen. Whatever the outcome, the brand is seen to be controversial, different and challenging. Perhaps another more tangible manifestation of physique is that of the 'tone of voice': how the brand speaks to the customer or recipient of any particular communication. Thus most people perceive Coca-Cola as youthful, energetic, positive, well intentioned because of the tone, style and nature of the communications that the company puts out. Coke 'owns' the imagery, the song, the bottle shape and the youthful energy. The RNLI by contrast is perceived as robust, reliable, always there in an emergency, strong, rugged and dependable. Everything that they do reinforces that perception and delivers a particular tone or physical presence to its various audiences.

Brand presentation (the outside appearance), the way packaging, advertising and promotion represents the brand to the public, is perhaps the most visible of the three Ps. Retail outlets clearly need to convey the values espoused by their parent organisation, hence the appearance and even feeling inside a Tesco store is very different to that in a branch of Marks & Spencer. Intel 'own' the four note signature used for every PC advertisement so that it is recognisable even on the radio. Charity shops similarly need to reflect their charity's brand values accurately. Sue Ryder shops demonstrate the thrift, economy and compassion espoused by their founder, and a move 'up market' would endanger the brand perception of shop volunteers and customers alike. On the other hand, Oxfam's specialisation into books and furniture in some of its shops more comfortably fits with the educational and developmental aspirations and values of the charity. Likewise the representation of some Oxfam specialist outlets to retail more fashionable items and accessories, at higher prices, reinforces the organisation's lead in charity retail and customers' ability to make valuable finds for themselves – whatever their particular needs are.

A good example of the way in which this analysis has been used is with the work that Arthritis Care undertook in developing its brand identity during the 1990s. As discussed in Chapter two, in 1983 the

charity changed its name (from 'The British
ritis Association') in order to reflect mor
supportive work, and to differentiate
only other national arthritis chari
research. Throughout the 1990s Arth
improving user involvement to become an o.
people rather than 'for' them. By 1999 the boa
majority of people with personal experience of a.
bers. The new name was retained but the strapline in .
'empowering people with arthritis'. To quote Richard Gu.
executive 1992–2001) 'The *care* in the name had changed fron.
*ing for* people with arthritis to *caring about* the issues that conce.
people with arthritis'. The refocus was and still is reflected in all
the organisation's communications, publications, policy work and
promotion, both internal and external.

# The power of brand values

Charities generally have distinct advantages when it comes to developing and communicating brand values. Changing the world is a
pretty big idea. Whether it is Friends of the Earth, who set out to
save the planet, or the Donkey Sanctuary, who set out to protect
donkeys from cruelty and enable them to have a happy old age,
ideas and values can be readily identified. In each case programmes
are developed to communicate these effectively to the organisation's chosen audiences.

## CASE STUDY **OXFAM**

The Oxford Committee for Famine Relief was set up in 1942 as one of a
number of groups in the UK aiming to highlight the problems created by
the Nazi occupation of Greece, requesting that relief be sent to those in
most urgent need. In 1943 the Oxford Committee for Famine Relief was
registered as a charity and its first appeal – 'Greek Week' – raised
£12,700 for the Greek Red Cross. This was a remarkable achievement if
you think that the brand was unknown, and people in war-torn Britain,
who were already undergoing rationing, were then being asked to give
funds to combat hunger in a far away theatre of the war.
Since then Oxfam has consistently pioneered advertising and
promotional methods, later adopted by other charities and the
commercial world alike. Its modern name, taken from the then 'Telex'
abbreviation of its longer name, was formally adopted in 1965, by which
time the brand was widely recognised as being authoritative, reliable, and
able to move quickly and effectively. During the 1960s and 1970s,
through the great work of Harold Sumption, considered by many to be
the 'father of modern fundraising,' Oxfam's brand values were presented

graphically through simple advertisements and direct mail. These used courier fonts to appear type written and urgent whilst simultaneously tapping into the public's conscience and goodwill. Oxfam is one of the few not-for-profit organisations to have taken the integration of its communications seriously. A consistent feel is present throughout their publications, print, Internet or advertising though the organisation admits that there is still a long way to go before their marketing can truly be considered integrated.

For-profit organisations have long understood the need to communicate consistent brand values and this is clearly seen in the example provided by Scottish Widows. Financial service marketing has similarities to the marketing of many charities in that the services offered are intangible, often not actively sought and rarely fully understood by customers. Despite this, the use of the 'Scottish Widow' (literally represented by a young attractive female figure dressed in a long black cloak) for several years in all advertising, sales promotion, publications and other marketing materials has created a trust within the public's mind second to none according to the managing director of Citigate Albert Frank advertising agency Jeremy Prescott. He says: 'As financial service companies go Scottish Widows have established a clarity and confidence that speaks volumes for keeping the messages simple.' He continues, 'too many not-for-profit organisations still haven't understood the value of the brands they own and the need to communicate simple, consistent messages to the public in order to create, firstly awareness, secondly understanding and then, and only then, empathy with the cause.'

This is very reminiscent of the sales mnemonic AIDA which very usefully reminds us that it is essential, within any sales cycle, to create:

- attention;
- interest;
- desire, and finally
- action.

The many attempts to shorten or short circuit this cycle may have occasional success but will rarely provide sustained activity over the long term. The acronym is a very useful one for any communicators to use to remind themselves that proper communication and understanding is a process that can rarely be reduced to a single message or campaign.

# Creating ownership

While, as Oxfam illustrates, brand values can be one of the most powerful elements in modern charity marketing, unless they are lived and realised daily by those individuals who work within or support an organisation, such values are empty and worthless. Ownership is the key to realising the power of a brand, and charities must work as hard, if not harder, than commercial organisations to achieve buy-in of brand values at all levels.

As with those companies in service industries, where staff meet or deal with customers every day, so it is the volunteers and staff within charities, those who work at the real grass roots, who are positioned to hold the greatest brand equity. In fact, charities should bring a variety of stakeholders into establishing their brand if the process is to be a success. This includes staff and 'working' volunteers, but also senior volunteers such as trustees, donors and service-users or beneficiaries who should also be consulted. Every individual attached to an organisation has a particular perspective on the brand values that they perceive and that have attracted them to support a particular cause.

One useful exercise in developing a brand and its inherent values is to bring a cross-section of these stakeholders together, inviting representatives from each group on the strength of their ability to champion the eventually emerging brand among their peers and colleagues. Once brought together in this way, stakeholders can be asked to share their views on the organisation, with questions that encourage creative expression, such as 'if the organisation was an animal, what sort of animal would it be'. While that type of question may sound frivolous, it will get people talking and should reveal valuable insights into how individuals view a particular cause, allowing participants to express their emotional response to an organisation in a tangible way that can be readily understood.

If holding a meeting of stakeholders or a series of smaller focus groups is not feasible, or the views of a much larger group of individuals are required, then a paper survey can prove a useful alternative. A questionnaire can be mailed to as many people as the budget permits, provided sufficient resources are available to collate and analyse the responses when they come back. The drawback of a paper survey is that some participants will perceive it as remote and impersonal, and more likely to suggest that an organisation is simply paying lip service to involving individuals in the development of a brand. For this reason, care should be taken in constructing the questions of a survey, and it should be made clear at the outset what weight and influence respondents will have within the overall process.

Whatever methods are used to involve stakeholders, it is unlikely that the brand values that emerge will be totally alien or unexpected to anybody. Brands are a distillation of the attitudes, perceptions and values that come from within an organisation, and anyone who works for or supports a particular cause should have some empathy with those attitudes and values. Of course, in the charitable context, a brand also has to be consistent with the established legal objects of the respective organisation. Any brand values that are imposed from outside a charity will not only seem alien to stakeholders, who could immediately reject any sense of ownership, those values are also likely to be intrinsically false.

Once understanding of the brand has been developed through consultation, part of the process of achieving wider ownership involves effective internal communication throughout the charity. As stated earlier, those individuals involved at the start of the process, when the brand values have been distilled, should be urged and expected to serve as brand champions within their stakeholder groups. In this way, a respected and well connected volunteer – who has helped to define a charity's brand – can then use his or her own personal and professional networks to explain how those values have been arrived at, what the brand stands for and how other volunteers can help to implement it.

This type of approach will be much more successful than an edict from the senior management team, or trustee body, that simply states 'this is our brand' and expects everyone immediately to buy into the end product. A more likely result of this approach will be to disenfranchise vast numbers of people from the entire brand development process; they will never believe, and therefore never communicate, the brand values in their work. Internal communication vehicles such as newsletters, team briefings and even conferences can be used to reinforce brand values, ideally calling on examples of how the brand is being realised at various levels of the charity, but this should not be seen as a replacement for more personal communication and endorsement. Above all, it is critically important that trustees and any senior management team sign up to the brand at the outset, and are seen publicly to espouse and fulfil the brand values. Too many senior figures in charities pay scant regard to their brand, believing it has little to do with their concerns, which may rest in operations, resources or finance. However, this lack of engagement is very quickly detected by staff and volunteers, who may themselves be sceptical of the brand development process and its outcomes. The absence of endorsement from the top of any organisation usually signals the failure of an initiative, and never more so than when establishing or reinforcing a brand that must run through every level of a charity to be successful.

# A step too far?

Having established a strong and clearly defined brand, it is then a logical next step for some organisations to extend that brand into other areas and markets, reaching more and wider audiences. Such a move should, of course, be consistent with the marketing strategy. Too many charities, and their commercial counterparts, see market share as an end in itself. It is not, and if a charity's strategy clearly identifies a single, highly targeted audience, it can be wasting time, money and other valuable resources in taking its brand elsewhere, at least until it has achieved the aims of its original strategy.

If a charity's marketing strategy does allow or require the extension of its brand, there are several ways in which this may be pursued. One increasingly popular commercial model is the transference of established brands into areas of operation with which they have not previously been associated. Perhaps the most prevalent of these areas is in financial services, where some of the strongest retailing brands – from Tesco to Marks & Spencer – have attempted to sell banking and investment products to existing and new customers. There is a synergy here between possessing the desire to purchase and possessing the means to purchase. However, this has not made the marketing of financial products successful for all companies, and some are already withdrawing from the market, acknowledging that they have little experience in offering financial services, and that their customers do not see necessarily see their familiar brands as belonging in this field.

When it comes to diversification of a brand, there can be few examples, in the UK or indeed anywhere, greater than that of Virgin. Originally established as a record label in the early 1970s, the Virgin brand has been extended into an enormous range of markets, from soft drinks and clothing manufacture to airline and rail operations, and now even financial services. In all these markets, the figure of Richard Branson has loomed large, for within Virgin Branson is seen as the epitome of the companies' brand values, standing for trust, entrepreneurship and innovation. It is perhaps too early to say if Virgin's aggressive forays into new markets have been an overall success or failure. Certainly there have been notable problems, perhaps the greatest being that of Virgin Trains.

Here the brand was applied to an existing service over which Virgin had little real influence beyond surface decoration and window dressing. Virgin's brand values of entrepreneurship, innovation and reliability have therefore experienced an uncomfortable ride.

Few charities have attempted brand diversification on Virgin's scale. One example that does stand out is Charity Projects, with its Comic Relief brand. In fact, it might be argued that here the charity has achieved far greater success with its 'Red Nose' activities than its commercial counterparts have managed. Clothing, music, books and fashion accessories have all conveyed the Comic Relief brand, and managed to remain consistent with the values of the main biannual fundraiser, providing fun in a socially responsible manner. Breakthrough Breast Cancer has also achieved similar success, if on a smaller scale, with its own forays into clothing, music and fashion events. The 'fit' has been deemed apposite and accepted by the consumer.

There are other routes to diversification that have proved more attractive in recent years, often due to their accessibility and low financial risk to the charity. Cause-related marketing, from event sponsorship through to elaborate charity of the year schemes, have involved companies and not-for-profits in many high profile brand marriages, intended to boost sales to the company and attract new supporters for the charity. While there have been some highly successful fits – for example Tesco and its Computers for Schools initiative, and Walkers with the similarly branded Books for Schools – the public has not always seen the logic behind these relationships. An example of the problem of brand discord can be found in HelpAd, an initiative of the International Red Cross Movement in the mid-1990s. This was a highly ambitious scheme, which involved the brokering of partnerships between mutually beneficial brands such as Hovis and Marmite. Manufacturers would join in on-pack promotions, donating the monetary value of this advertising to the Red Cross Movement. But beyond the companies involved, there was no brand synergy that aligned these manufacturers and their highly commercial products with the care services and international aid provided by the Red Cross. Unsurprisingly, the public failed to take the promotion to its heart, and the scheme was quietly dropped.

Similar cases of brand dissonance can be found in the commercial sector. Pret A Manger is a recent example, a brand synonymous with quality food, aimed at an informed, professional consumer. There was hostility from both the media and the public when the company sold a minority shareholding to McDonalds, a brand tarnished over many years by damaging allegations over its manufacturing processes. The deal was doubtless struck on financial grounds, providing Pret A Manger with extra capital investment, but the longer-term damage to Pret's brand equity is yet to be evaluated.

There are other avenues to brand extension and development that can prove less contentious. Partnerships behind the Children's Promise (a consortium of children's charities) and Will Aid (a consortium of international aid charities) along with recent high profile mergers such as that of Terrence Higgins Trust and the London Lighthouse, mark another emerging trend in the voluntary sector. Again, the rationale behind these initiatives is doubtless sound – minimising or cutting back on expenditure while hopefully maximising the fundraising potential of such partnerships – but the effect on the brand values and loyalty of participating charities should not be underestimated. The Children's Promise may have encouraged Britain's workforce to donate an hour's salary to 'children's charities', but how many individuals taking part engaged directly with the specific brands of participating charities? The likes of the NSPCC and Barnardo's have spent many years attempting to differentiate their work and their brand values in the eyes of the public. Activities such as the Children's Promise would have done little to support that effort beyond creating some short-term effect on their bottom line.

The lesson here, as shown in all these examples, is for charities to apply just as rigorous an analysis to any new market and marketing initiative as they have to those they traditionally operate in. Once a robust marketing strategy and a clear brand identity have been established and bought into at all levels of an organisation, this should not be ignored at the first sign of a potentially large cheque. Any proposal to associate with third party brands must be evaluated to see if the respective brand values match. Without this, the risk of brand dissonance and, often, public failure is too great for charities reasonably to take.

# Brand recognition and loyalty

Some of the best known brands in the UK are charities. According to the Future Foundation's 'Charity Communications Monitor' (a syndicated quarterly survey of spontaneous and prompted awareness among the public in the UK) the NSPCC scores over 96 per cent prompted awareness whilst the British Red Cross scores 99 per cent. This is comparable to global brands like Coca-Cola and McDonalds who spend £10s of millions each year to advertise and promote their corporate brands.

---

**CASE STUDY   GREAT ORMOND STREET HOSPITAL**

As Marion Allford (1993) explains, the successful Great Ormond Street appeal is a useful example of how a major capital appeal can also be used as a brand-building device. GOSH was already probably one of the best known in the UK hospitals in London. Following the successful appeal which raised £53 million the hospital is certainly the best known in the UK (excluding perhaps 'Holby General' in the BBC television soap *Casualty*). The key lesson one can learn from this is that the meticulous three years of planning included very careful analysis of the brand's strengths and weaknesses, and built upon these attributes to persuade all sections of society to buy into the importance and urgency of helping GOSH.

Years on, the fundraising team still receive many unsolicited gifts and offers of fundraising activities because people believe in the brand and the value of offering help.

---

Recognition however certainly does not guarantee loyalty. French Connection in the UK have been running their controversial FCUK advertising campaign for some time. Like Benetton before them, they achieve a lot of media coverage, comment and awareness. The question remains however as to whether French Connection are really doing much to add value to their brand and gain increased loyalty from their customers. The dissonance between the 'in your face' irreverent campaign and the experience of shopping in an FCUK store is considerable.

In commercial marketing, customer loyalty to the brand is crucial where a premium is sought and where repeat purchases are vital to sales growth and profitability. For charities, brand loyalty is something different. Donors have favourite causes, and users often become donors themselves, particularly at the end of their life through a legacy. Why would anybody write a charity into his or her will – unless perhaps to annoy or spite the family – without a sense of loyalty to that charity's brand? Customer care is clearly very relevant, but how does the charity brand gain loyalty?

An analysis of donor behaviour, using an onion construct (see Figure 12) may be helpful in this context. On the outside is behaviour: how we act or react in response to a given stimulus. Underneath are our attitudes, which clearly have an effect on our behaviour. Under those attitudes lie our beliefs: the things we hold to be true or at least have faith in. Thus whilst one can change behaviour through superficial stimulation and persuade someone to buy (or give), it is more effective to obtain a change of attitude which will then radically impact behaviour. Better still is to address the inner-most beliefs. This is, of course, the hardest task, which is why the Jesuits said 'give me the child at six and I'll give you the man'. How-ever, where a charity is unable to place itself anywhere within an individual's belief structure, any support given will, at best, be tran-sitory and subject to change.

**FIGURE 12** A MODEL ILLUSTRATING THE RELATIONSHIP BETWEEN HUMAN BEHAVIOUR AND BELIEFS

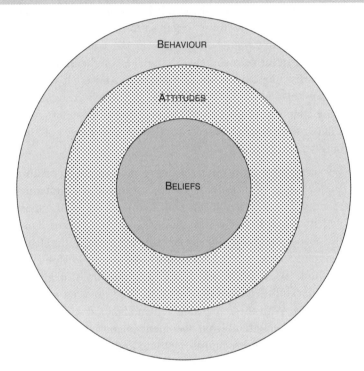

We see this in peer pressure, particularly among younger con-sumers; 'Cabbage Patch Dolls' gave way to 'Teenage Mutant Ninja Turtles' who themselves then fell before the might of the 'Teletub-bies'. Adult behaviours are little different. It may be important per-haps to be seen at the Mcmillan Cancer Ball, but unless those supporters actually share the values espoused by the organisation – its vision and mission – it is unlikely that they will ever do more than buy tickets to the next event. This may be fine in the short term but where is the impetus to write that charity into those sup-porters wills going to come from?

# Conveying the brand

Brands may be manifested in many ways – through customer experiences, through product development, through advertising – but one of the most effective ways to convey a brand is through a strong corporate identity. Corporate identity provides a short cut to brand values than can transcend language, religions and international boundaries. As we have seen, global surveys of the world's biggest brands will usually feature Coca-Cola and McDonalds in two of the top three slots and the third is normally occupied by the Red Cross. All three of these organisations stand for very clear and understandable values; anywhere in the world, Coca Cola can be relied upon for refreshment, McDonalds for cheap fast food, and the Red Cross for care without questions. And each of these 'superbrands' also possesses a distinctive and widely recognised logo, utilising shape, characters and colours. The number of people around the world who do not recognise the 'golden arches' of McDonalds is surely falling rapidly.

Corporate identity is often misinterpreted simply to mean an organisation's logo. Certainly, logos are an important component of any identity, but they are just one of many elements, the most basic of which also include colours, typestyles and straplines. For example, the corporate identity of the British Red Cross is the distinctive red cross on a clear white background; the use of carefully selected red (Pantone 032), white and black as a minimum in all publications and marketing, including its website; and the typefaces Bembo and Helvetica. With these few simple elements, a distinct identity can be extended through internal documents, external advertising and posters, fundraising brochures, clothing and vehicles, providing points of consistency whatever the variance in messages and audience.

However, corporate identity extends beyond such simple signifiers. It is also embodied in how an organisation presents itself in words and images. Images can be used to highlight the positive aspects of a cause, portraying beneficiaries with respect as individuals who have control over their lives. Alternatively, some charities focus on images of despair and of desperate need. Both approaches may be valid to certain organisations, but each will influence the way in which individuals perceive and interact with the brand. So too can a choice of words. For example, Leonard Cheshire ensures that the language in its marketing and communications protects the dignity of its service users. It does not talk about the disabled, an amorphous group who need help, but rather refers constantly to disabled people, individuals who face challenges in society and to whom the charity offers constructive help.

As has been stated earlier, implementing brands effectively is critical if the values and equity in those brands are to be maintained. Many large companies are fortunate in having dedicated marketing departments and professionals at all levels and locations within an organisation, which can maintain certain standards in how the brand is projected.

In charities, such resources are rarely, if ever, available. Brands are constantly interpreted and conveyed by staff and volunteers whose day-to-day job is delivering direct charitable services, and volunteers are usually working outside normal management lines. Regulating the use of a brand in these circumstances can be very difficult, if not impossible. Marketing materials might be produced by dozens of individuals to varying standards. The best solution is, usually, to be as supportive as possible. If volunteers and local staff are involved in establishing an organisation's brand values, as outlined earlier, they should possess a sense of ownership and understand the importance of that brand, both to themselves and the cause they support. If it is then made easy for them to adopt the brand – providing templates for marketing materials, copies of logos and fonts in multiple electronic formats, that can be imported into the most basic word processing or desktop publishing programs – they will have little reason to deviate from this.

Above all, lead by example. Ensure that all centrally organised marketing activities are true to the brand, and illustrate well how the brand can be conveyed effectively to different audiences in different circumstances. Once those in the field see what can be achieved through adherence to the brand, they will soon want to follow suit without the need for much coaxing from the centre. And the more that local initiatives can reinforce brand values, the more successful national activities will be in distinguishing the cause from the competition.

Naturally, corporate identities may be required to change over time, particularly if a change of charity name is also being considered. Quite often this means retaining the traditional name for legal purposes, but trading under a new name. In this way, the Royal National Lifeboat Institution streamlined its brand from the well-known initials RNLI to, simply, Lifeboats.

A more drastic name change was undertaken by The Spastics Society, when it adopted the new title of Scope in the mid-1990s. This was as a consequence of the word 'spastic' becoming increasingly used as a term of abuse and service users demanded change. The danger of losing awareness by changing name was far outweighed by the potential damage to the charity's brand values – caring for those with cerebral palsy – if it continued to trade under the old name. Total public awareness did indeed drop from over 90 per cent for The Spastics Society to under 50 per cent for the new Scope. By 2001 this had recovered to 71 per cent and whilst the organisation acknowledges that it is unlikely ever to enjoy the previous high levels, it regards the gains in retained brand values and support as far outweighing that loss. The stated cost of the complete change was something over £3 million but the real cost in lost donations, lost position and understanding during the intervening years could well have been double that (Hewson 1997). This cost perhaps pales into insignificance when compared to the Royal Mail débâcle upon spending £5 million to change its name to Consignia. It had to bear all the costs of changing back less than two years later, following massive media criticism and the admission by their new chief executive that the exercise had been a very costly mistake.

# Conclusion

We can see how the brand has in many organisations become synonymous with the entire offering, encompassing product, values and everything perceived by customers and users. However in many not-for-profit organisations, and still quite a few major companies, brand values are at odds with those espoused by the organisation and thus public perception is equally inconsistent. Worse still, when employees and supporters do not feel ownership of shared values it is likely that further confusion and brand fragmentation will arise.

Careful marketing planning can do much to avoid this, but once again integration of those plans, throughout the organisation, is crucial to success. It may be helpful within not-for-profit organisations, as Joe Saxton suggests, to substitute the word 'reputation' everywhere one might otherwise talk of 'brand' to volunteers and non-marketing staff. Rebranding is an exercise to be carried out only after very careful consideration of all the alternatives – but it can, if there is no alternative, help to meet changed objectives and public perceptions.

# CHAPTER FIVE

# Shareholder versus stakeholder

'There is no formula for success. But there is a formula for failure and that is to try and please everybody.'    *Nicholas Ray*

'Pay no attention to what the critics say, no statue has ever been put up to a critic.'    *Jean Sibelius*

This chapter looks at the many audiences that organisations of all types must consider in their marketing activities. It explores how marketing takes place in charities through the conduits of service users and donors, and looks at the development and impact of customer loyalty schemes within both commercial organisations and charities. The differences in the make up and attitudes of key groups defined as stakeholders and shareholders are contrasted and conclusions are drawn about some crucial differences but also some surprising degrees of overlap.

## Shareholders

It is true that one of the first 'laws' of business is that profit must be made. But for whom, and over what timeframe? Equally, whilst most charities would agree that their role is, in some way, to change the status quo, they cannot do that unless they generate sufficient funds to achieve their objectives over time. In order to survive in a fiercely competitive world they are, in reality, compelled to generate surpluses, profits by any other name, so that they can plan ahead, remain solvent and able to deploy their resources and energy effectively. Thus the question is not so much profits versus change for good as how the profits are deployed and, importantly, who has a real say in the way that those surpluses are generated and dispersed. In essence then both types of organisation seek long-term survival and are dependent upon a range of stakeholders to ensure that survival. As Ansoff (1968) says, for companies 'long-term profitability results from a commitment to understanding the political and social fabric of a community'. This chapter explores the similarities and differences between both types of organisation and examines more closely how each achieves success.

In a Help the Aged survey some years ago shareholders were asked about their investing preferences. In particular shareholders were asked whether, if return on investment was broadly similar, which they would prefer: to invest in companies that had a well developed and publicly recognised community affairs programme, supporting charities and other not-for-profit organisations or to invest in companies who put all efforts into maximising profits. The overwhelming majority clearly preferred to invest in companies seen to be operating in socially responsible ways. Opinions expressed implied approval for these companies and an expectation that they would be better employers with a longer-term view of business development.

# Stakeholders

It is generally recognised today that organisations need to consider not just their shareholders or effective owners, but everyone who has an interest, a stake, in their success. These audiences broadly split into two main types:

- internal groupings, including employees, management, the board and volunteers (where they exist);
- external groupings, including customers, users, investors, supporters and prospects.

In addition, of course, there are the opinion-influencers such as media commentators, trade institutions and umbrella bodies. Interestingly other surveys along the lines of the Help the Aged research but asking customers similar questions about their preferences for brands supporting community investment have had very similar results. They indicate clearly a strong public preference in the UK for organisations seen to be acting responsibly with society's interests in mind rather than for those with the more limited horizon of maximising shareholder value.

In fact of course, taking a long-term view of organisational survival, it is not only desirable but probably essential to operate with the public's approval, support and goodwill in order to ensure that all stakeholders, as far as possible, feel some ownership of the organisation. Ownership can take many forms from the 100 per cent shareholding chief executive and chairman of a family business to the individual donor who feels in tune with and a small part of a charity. This sense of participation however, when widely dispersed, can only help sustain the organisation in the long term.

---

CASE STUDY **NDCS**

The case of NDCS (the National Deaf Children's Society) illustrates the importance of ownership and participation well. Formed, as a self-help group, in 1944 by parents of deaf children the charity now has nearly 14,000 members and works with 34,000 deaf and hard of hearing children. Shared experiences are enormously beneficial to the organisation and the various participant groups of stakeholders: deaf children, parents, and supporters. Mark Astarita, the deputy chief executive, agrees that a cohesive marketing approach is vital but wonders if in fact many do it by accident. 'We already come over as a warm caring, family orientated organisation. Is the corporate sector borrowing our clothes?' he asks, and continues: 'By keeping the messages simple for donors, they can feel that they really are making a difference.' Astarita believes that charities are playing an increasingly important role for people in that as religious observances and practices decline the need for the feel good factor becomes even more important for supporters, donors and volunteers alike.

The charity plans an international service providing a global challenge by working with overseas partners as a real increase in meeting the needs of deaf children. Astarita adds: 'If this had been a solely fundraising driven initiative we'd have done it three years ago.' However careful consultation with all interested stakeholders and a proactive approach to ensure a sense of ownership has taken far longer though the benefits of an integrated approach are he admits, 'well worth waiting for'.

An interesting example of the interaction between not-for-profit and corporate has been the longevity of a relationship between NDCS and HSBC. The bank selected three main charities to work with and the areas covered were the elderly, homelessness and disability. With Age Concern and Shelter occupying the slots in the first two areas NDCS was by some way the smallest of the chosen organisations. Despite this the initial three-year collaboration was extend by two years and then again by a further year. Why? Astarita believes it was down to the match; 'a perfect fit' he says. The bank got involved from the chair down to staff at local branch level and this participation and commitment made the relationship 'come alive'.

---

In the refocus of its objects to the provision of mobility support for blind people GDBA (Guide Dogs for the Blind) may have achieved a similar impact for donors and potential supporters. Formerly the charity was seen simply as a provider of guide dogs for blind people. Unfortunately only some 4,000 people could be helped in this way at any one time leading to an enormous gulf between public perceptions and the reality of service provision. Media stories about the charity's substantial reserves exacerbated the situation. The refocus and dramatic broadening of the organisation's work coincides with a much more proactive approach to fundraising to address both the deficits which the charity had been running, partly in an attempt to address criticisms of its reserves, and to fund the expanded nature and scope of the work. This revised picture should enable the organisation to work more closely with groups of stakeholders, especially donors, and create a platform for development in the twenty-first century.

## CASE STUDY **RNLI**

RNLI has also faced the issue of large perceived reserves and the need to reconcile highly effective fundraising with changing public perceptions. Ian Ventham, the former head of fundraising, helped to persuade the charity of the opportunity it had to broaden its work which would, coincidentally, improve further the fundraising proposition. Thus, whilst the core mission remains to provide a lifeboat service to save life at sea, the RNLI has taken on the additional tasks of beach rescue (lifeguarding), rescue services on inland waters, and help with flood relief, both in the UK and Ireland, and overseas.

These new tasks have not been without difficulties and challenges. A conservative supporter base had to be persuaded that the new activities did not detract from the traditional and much respected work of the lifeboat crews. Beach Rescue brought with it the challenge of working with local authorities and in partnership with two established charities in the lifeguarding field, Royal Lifesaving Society, and Surf Life Saving Association. Sending a rapid response team to Mozambique in 2001 brought the organisation into contact with DFID for the first time.

Working on inland waters and in flood relief situations in UK and Ireland challenged traditional ways of working, and highlighted different training needs for crews. Crucially some of these new activities required the RNLI to amend its governing document, its Royal Charter.

Perhaps the biggest challenge, though, was to plan and execute complex internal and external marketing and communication strategies to explain, justify and sell the expanding role of the charity. The stakeholders ranged from trustees to crew members, and from Charity Commission to district councils. This process is far from over.

In each of these cases the organisations have endeavoured to make their cause come alive for new and existing stakeholder groups which in turn provides greater support and improved services to the beneficiary groups. These are example of the virtuous circle of communications, where change well executed and communicated further impacts communications, which in turn assist the change process.

# The role of the consumer

One of the things marketeers need to do in order to understand the various agendas and interests held by differing groups of stakeholders is to become one of that group. Through understanding can come strategies for developing and improving approval. Commercial organisations frequently invest in 'professional shoppers', 'mystery customers' and unannounced visits/inspections to try to gauge and mirror customer reactions to the buying experience. Fundraisers can gain very valuable donor experiences by becoming one. Using a false name if necessary, it is very instructive to be on the receiving end of communications, sometimes apparently endless, from your own charity. Similarly, try buying something from one of your own shops or outlets or participate, as a punter, in an organised fundraising or sponsorship activity. This approach can be taken further: try to experience the customer care of rival or at least other charities operating within the same sector. Valuable feedback is available and comparisons can be made in order to improve your own charity's organisational responses, communications and received perceptions.

An important difference between many for-profit and not-for-profit organisations is that the end user or consumer is quite different to the actual purchaser or customer. For example Leonard Cheshire's customers are generally local authorities and health trusts whilst the service users are a wide range of disabled people. Clearly whilst social work staff should be working closely with their clients, the authority's priorities may be quite different to those of the disabled people themselves. The charity can become the 'aunt sally' stuck in the middle trying to deliver services that the service users want, appropriate support where and when they want it, whilst the cash-strapped purchasers are seeking to minimise costs and the resources to be expended on the support. Mutually incompatible priorities are hard to reconcile but marketeers must put themselves in the shoes of both groups if they are to develop a clear understanding in order to improve what they do themselves.

# Customers as advocates

It is well recognised that genuine testimonials from satisfied customers have always been a valuable part of establishing credibility in the minds of prospective customers or clients. Anecdotal evidence suggests that whilst a satisfied customer might, unprompted, recommend the product or service to perhaps six or eight acquaintances, dissatisfied customers tell 20 or more – underlining the need to build upon and actively use the experiences of clients who are content with the experience they have received.

Fundraisers have the opportunity to go a step further. Provided that a not-for-profit is meeting the needs of its service users, their experiences can be used very positively to underpin a fundraising approach. Whether it is photographs of rescued animals or the quotations from beneficiaries who have positive messages the impact can be similarly powerful. Equally there is no need to descend into the 'triumph over tragedy' outdated models of charity fundraising. Honest, positive experiences can be used with much greater effect though much more work in developing and recording those experiences will be needed.

## CASE STUDY **ARTHRITIS CARE**

Arthritis Care spent a significant amount of time and energy in developing internal guidelines for the use, within the direct marketing programme, of user experiences. It is easy, but very short-sighted, to fall into the trap of using 'heroes in adversity' stories which, although initially attention-grabbing, demean the users themselves and often, over time, turn donors and potential supporters away from the very cause seeking help.

Instead the charity developed a four-point check list that any message coming from fundraising needed to be, positive, honest, powerful and urgent. Powerful urgent messages were needed to change perceptions of the 'non-life threatening' 'just a symptom of old age' nature of arthritis. Positive did not mean that the full impact of severe arthritis in childhood could not be portrayed, but that the outcomes would be a key part of the message to avoid turning people with arthritis into 'victims'. Honesty was also crucial to avoid promising a cure but showing how information, empowerment and the right support can make all the difference to someone who has arthritis – at any age.

The impact over time was significant; more users accepted the validity of the advertising, communications and fundraising activities and were willing to be portrayed themselves. In turn this lead to a greater understanding by supporters and an uplift in long-term support.

Cancer charities have been adopting a similar approach with much greater emphasis on the long-term impacts of interventions on those overcoming cancer to persuade donors to give on a long-term basis. It was the threat of death which until recently was the big scare factor that mobilised millions of people to give hundreds of millions of pounds towards cancer research and care. The recent turnaround is neatly summed up in the quote used in press and direct response television advertising (DRTV) that having cancer is about life, not death. The lessons relevant to for-profit organisations lie in the life affirming nature of such projects and the value that can be added to commercial brands and ventures through working with appropriate not-for-profit organisations. Positive attitudes and experiences are reflected in enhanced values and reputations.

# The power of investors

Within commercial organisations investors are usually shareholders who expect a reasonable return on investment through stock dividends and growth in share values. As we have seen, however, those same investors can value highly other attributes such as an organisation's contribution to its local community.

Shareholders can exert enormous power upon a board of directors, particularly in cases where acquisitions and mergers come into play. Large shareholders, usually institutional (and often pension funds) are courted and kept well informed as to the intentions and plans of the organisation. This preoccupation with share value is not always a healthy one when, as in the case of Worldcom, Enron and Xerox it leads to fraudulent declarations of profits in order to maintain inflated share values.

In charities donors are sometimes seen more as a company's shareholders than customers of a particular not-for-profit. They provide much of the funding for the work of the organisation and fundraising departments are charged with maintaining good relations, keeping them well informed and happy with the work of the charity. However there is a potential dissonance. Donors receive no dividends, yet without their continued incoming investment the charity will (usually) run out of funds all too soon. The cultivation therefore of long-term supporters as investors as opposed to regarding them simply as customers can be very helpful to the survival and long-term health of a not-for-profit organisation. Lessons from the good practices of commercial organisations need to be learned and adopted in suitable formats to fit the differing attitudes, perceptions and needs of donors over shareholders.

Increasingly the communications function within a company will include responsibility for investor relations, often under the guise of corporate affairs. Meetings and briefings for larger institutional investors will be augmented by improved shareholder communications rather than relying simply on the annual report and accounts, the AGM and dividends, interim or final. Great effort is made to ensure that the press is briefed ahead of profit forecasts or warnings. Takeovers, mergers and acquisitions present particular challenges for companies to inform investors effectively, building confidence, understanding and feelings of shared ownership.

## Communicating with investors

Good fundraisers already spend much time talking to donors in an effort to understand how they want to hear about the charity's progress but almost inevitably those charged with direct marketing cannot resist adding an additional 'ask' to donor communication, however soft, however polite. Whilst in the past this may have raised the number of unprompted donations there is a real risk of alienating long-term supporters, permanently. 'They only ever write to me for money' is an all too familiar response to communications, especially welcome packs, beloved of direct marketing agencies for creating instant uplifts for minimal investment.

The ubiquitous charity questionnaire, apparently asking for a supporter's (or potential supporter's) views but in reality a donor recruitment or enhancement device, is one piece of DM still in widespread use but perhaps nearing the end of its useful life due to overuse and misuse. A recent Mcmillan Cancer door-drop includes a letter from the chief executive asking for help so that the organisation understands, ' ... a little bit about you and your experiences on cancer care ... ' it then goes on to ask for a modest gift of £2 per month. A banker's order is attached to the questionnaire. The inevitable free pen is enclosed. The ask is made despite the recipient being a long-term, occasional, supporter of the charity. It is acknowledged of course that this is a cold recruitment pack seeking first time support, but how much more effective might it be to make a request for support *after* receipt of the returned questionnaire; the monetary request could then be accompanied by feedback on the results of the survey and an explanation of how these results will be used within the organisation. If supporters' views are genuinely sought, valued and used to determine policy, making an immediate request for money to accompany answers must significantly reduce response rates, even if the initial return on investment is much higher.

Despite the shortcomings of this particular communication – which in similar forms is used by dozens of major charities in their fundraising programmes – it is fair to comment that Mcmillan Cancer has an enviable reputation for its efforts to engage donors and enlist active support. Judy Beard, director of fundraising at the charity comments, 'we feel the pack has served its purpose and are testing alternative propositions with a view to replacing it as soon as we can find a viable replacement'.

By contrast a Friends of the Earth door-drop, signed by their chief executive Charles Secret, cuts straight to the point – it's the cheapest, most effective way of talking to people about urgent issues needing regular donations to help make a difference. The pen is still there as an 'uplift device' but it feels a much more honest, open approach. In the same vein a door-drop from CRUK includes a pen to help fill in the response form but is completely transparent, having asked on the outer envelope, 'how much does it cost to litter your doorstep?' The letter then goes on to admit that the cost to send the unaddressed letter is 13p and continues justifying that investment with refreshing candour.

Probably one of the worst examples around currently is from the World Villages for Children, an American organisation fundraising very successfully in the UK by sending addressed cold packs with 1 2p actually stuck on the letter. The letter goes on to ask for the recipient to add £10 and send back £10.12 p to feed a child for a week. The marketing director, when taxed upon the honesty and ethical nature of this type of approach, could only retreat behind a barrage of 'but it works' rhetoric. Perhaps in this context a much more effective piece of genuine supporter/investor communication would be a questionnaire aimed at understanding how the supporter actually wants to hear from the charity. As we have seen, Botton Village, a project for people with learning difficulties did this with enormous success. Having asked supporters whether they wanted to hear, once, twice, four times, twelve times per year, or whatever, the fundraisers then made sure that communications, fundraising or otherwise, fitted the requested pattern.

The Internet is providing innovative cost effective ways of enhancing investor communications. Oxfam has spent significant time and effort establishing which supporters prefer to receive E-mail information – and how often. Fundraising asks made as a part of an overall communications plan should produce better results over time even if initial returns on investment are lower. Charities must be particularly mindful of the need to satisfy supporters. It is only through long-term support from donors happy with what the organisation is achieving, and who feel part of or some ownership of its cause, that the charities themselves will succeed with the legacy development programmes which form a crucial part of an increasing number of fundraising strategies.

# Creating ownership

In developing ownership of a cause, a brand, and its inherent values it is useful, as already discussed, to bring a cross-section of stakeholders together, inviting representatives from each group on the strength of their ability to champion the emerging values among their peers and colleagues. Once brought together in this way, stakeholders can be asked to share their views on the organisation, allowing participants to express their emotional response to an organisation in a tangible, understandable way. For charities to put donors, service users, volunteers and staff in the same room might feel rather threatening. Properly facilitated however the results should prove invaluable and the resulting advocates are likely to energise many of their colleagues and friends.

Focus groups must be carefully structured and balanced. Thought must be given to the make-up and individual participants. If an experienced professional agency is not used then the facilitator must brief the group really carefully, ensuring agreement on the form and format. Enough time to allow participants to interact and engage is crucial if the group is to produce useful results. Meaningful feedback, of the results and their impact, for the individuals who were involved is an important but often overlooked vehicle to ensure continued support and to help develop brand champions.

Whilst paper surveys can prove a useful alternative, they cannot fully reproduce the emotional responses and feedback available through focus groups, or even informal feedback sessions. Once again all respondents must feel that their replies will genuinely influence the process. Whatever methods are used to involve stakeholders, it is unlikely that the values that emerge will be totally alien or unexpected to anybody. Charity causes, very like commercial brands, are a distillation of the attitudes, perceptions and values that come from within an organisation, and anyone who works for or supports a particular cause is likely to have great empathy with some if not all of those attitudes and values. Values that seem to be imposed from outside a charity will not only seem alien to stakeholders, who could immediately reject any sense of ownership but those values are likely to be intrinsically at odds with those perceived by the observers.

Work to develop brand champions needs to be based firmly on the results of empirical research such as that suggested rather than on the assumptions of those charged with fundraising or even on the input of trustees alone. At best an incomplete picture will result and at worst the risk of alienation and claims of outdated views or unworldly expectations are likely to result. Any communication plan should devote significant resources to the development and subsequent use of such brand champions. And this should include champions amongst the most senior of stakeholders, directors and trustees.

# The board

Chapter three draws attention to the need not only for thorough planning but also for the knowledge of those plans, and their implementation, to be fully communicated within the organisation. Too many marketing strategies and plans, excellent on paper, fail to get beyond first or second base because stakeholders (including crucially powerful stakeholders such as board members) lose confidence or allow other considerations to intrude during the inevitable refinement periods that follow a new programme or activity plan.

Naturally these 'second thoughts' are not confined to marketing programmes, but being a very visible manifestation of an organisation's intentions the implementation of marketing plans is likely to come under the most scrutiny and criticism. Boards of commercial and not-for-profit organisations are not driven purely by stated, and apparently agreed, corporate objectives. The case of British Airways' tailplanes is a good case in point. Agreement at a senior level to commission modern artists to repaint the tailplanes of the BA fleet, at significant cost, evaporated in the face of strident public criticism by the then Prime Minister, Margaret Thatcher. An even more costly reversion to union flag colours followed.

Not-for-profits are however even more likely to reject a marketing initiative prematurely if marketing continues to be seen as a 'bolt-on' and not really relevant to the world of charity.

Champions within the trustee body must be wholly behind new programmes of, say, fundraising investment. Typically, these are plans that will see a concerted increase in investment over four or five years, usually in an effort to improve the funding mix by reducing reliance on a single revenue source and increasing the availability of 'unrestricted' funds to allow the organisation to increase its investment in the provision of core services. Often such programmes produce negative cash flow over two or three years. It is then easy for boards who are not fully behind such programmes, or for influential individuals on those boards who do not fully understand their ramifications, to begin criticising, interfering and ultimately changing direction away from the agreed strategy. This will almost inevitably be at great cost to the organisation and allows a knee-jerk reaction in the face of criticism and ignorance to divert the charity from its purpose.

Senior managers have a responsibility to ensure unanimity of attitude towards such programmes; they must show resolution in the face of criticism. Preparation for, and contingency plans to counter, antipathy may be a very necessary part of the implementation process. When the NSPCC launched the 'Full stop campaign' they did so to the accompaniment of considerable media comment and voluntary sector scepticism. However internally everyone from the trustees and senior managers down to individual staff and volunteers working in all sections, service delivery, administration, finance and fundraising had bought into 'the big idea' the vision to put an end to child cruelty. So far, whilst external pundits carp about timescales and cost ratios, the organisation remains true to its purpose, evidence of clear and effective internal communications. Giles Pegram, the director responsible for the £250 million target, can take much of the credit for this. The model is worthy of replication.

# Conclusion

It can be seen from the preceding examples and descriptions that both commercial and not-for-profit organisations need stakeholder approval to operate most effectively. Careful consideration of who makes up this larger group is most important in considering the appropriate communications strategy to adopt.

Without this approval companies and charities will always struggle to communicate their values and ethos properly. Wilmott (2001) takes Ansoff's persuasive thesis further, and argues that the critical issue is that of a company's relationship with society. One very effective way to improve that relationship, the buy-in factor, is to promote closer working partnerships between for-profit and not-for-profit organisations who share values in their community involvement, corporate affairs and marketing activities. This is explored further in the next chapter.

# CHAPTER SIX

# Volunteers – the unique benefit proposition

'People who never get carried away should be.' *Malcolm Forbes*

'They laughed at Joan of Arc but she went right
ahead and built it.'                                      *Gracie Allan*

Volunteers are the very lifeblood of charities, and are one of the defining differences between for-profit and not-for-profit organisations. This chapter explores the unique input and involvement of volunteers in not-for-profit organisations and examines how they can play a vital part in any successful marketing approach. It shows how volunteers can become champions of brand values, which in turn reinforces the importance of internal leadership and commitment. Also examined is the fact that whilst in commercial organisations few employees would consider themselves as volunteers, many will volunteer as part of their company's community affairs programmes to work with not-for-profit organisations, which in turn can bring enormous benefits to both organisations.

## From supporter to volunteer

One of the overriding reasons why people support charities is their religious motivation. All the major religions teach the support and care of our neighbours. The word charity itself, derived from the Greek *caritas*, refers to love of our fellow man. Thus many charities have their roots in religious motivation, even if today they are secular in the way in which they operate.

Not-for-profit organisations with such origins do, of course, continue to derive wide scale support from their natural constituencies. Jewish Care for example, having been formed from 11 existing support and care charities working from Jewish roots looks to that community for much of its support even though its work is anything but constrained by religious or racial background. The propensity, therefore, to support not only through monetary gifts but by volunteered time remains high amongst those with active religious beliefs and continues to be a fertile source of volunteers for charities who can mobilise people through shared values.

---

**CASE STUDY  BROOKE HOSPITAL FOR ANIMALS**

The Brooke Hospital for Animals was founded in 1934 by Dorothy Brooke in response to the enormous suffering she saw first hand in Cairo (Searight 1993). She saw that thousands of ex-cavalry horses, sold off by the British Army at the end of the First World War, were still being literally worked to death 16 years later. She wrote a letter to the *Morning Post*, which brought in the equivalent of £20,000 to enable 'something to be done'. An attempt to provide care and support for these animals through an animal hospital and rest facility called 'The Cairo War Horse Memorial Hospital' rapidly expanded into a free veterinary service for working equines when the extent of the problems of poor animal care, ignorance and poverty were appreciated. The organisation now operates with 450 vets and staff in Egypt, Jordan, Pakistan, India and Afghanistan. Around one million treatments are administered each year and the charity has ambitious plans to quadruple that over the next five years through outreach and education projects. Typically supporters have very quietly given quite large amounts over extended periods of time, once they have visited one of the clinics. The motivation is prompted by a love of animals, in particular horses, donkeys and mules but there is evidence that a high percentage of active supporters, who participate in fundraising events and visits, are also active church goers. Thus the Brooke Hospital for Animals has, perhaps unknowingly, drawn enormous long-term support by finding synergy between the organisation's beliefs and values, and those of its supporters.

---

# Volunteers – stakeholders or shareholders?

Can volunteers be thought of as stakeholders and/or shareholders or do they need a different approach for support?

Ian Bruce (1998) usefully defines stakeholders as those who have rights and responsibilities over the running of a charity – thus strengthening the analogy with shareholders. However he goes on to say that therefore beneficiaries (and by extension volunteers) are not stakeholders in any legal or realistic sense. He adds obliquely however that *representatives* of beneficiaries, if recognised by the charity, are indeed stakeholders.

This is a limited view. In practical terms it would be much more helpful to consider all the involved groups – trustees, staff, beneficiaries, supporters, donors and volunteers – as stakeholders with an interest and investment, however intangible, in the organisation.

Certainly for communications planning volunteers need to be considered and thought of as having a real interest in what the organisation plans to do and how it executes its intentions.

# Founders as volunteers

Most businesses are started by an individual or small group of people who have a particular idea that might make money, or interest in an activity they are keen to attempt professionally. Sometimes it's even a vision about how things might be. When Steve Jobs and Steve Wozniak built the first Apple computers in their garage in 1976 they did not just have an idea they thought might make money. They foresaw the advantages of every home having a computer and this vision drove them on to seek venture capital from friends and build a business now worth billions of dollars worldwide.

In a not dissimilar way those driven to found charities do so usually from a deep conviction that a need must be met or the world changed in some way for the better. They 'volunteer' their services to this end.

---

CASE STUDY **LEONARD CHESHIRE**

Founding a charity was probably the last thing on Leonard Cheshire's mind in 1948. He was living at the time in a large, run-down country house trying to stave off bankruptcy after a failed venture. The matron of his local cottage hospital approached him and asked if he would consider giving a home to a man called Arthur Dykes, who was dying of liver cancer. Dykes had worked for a short time as a pigman with Cheshire in a self-sufficiency project. The matron told Cheshire that the doctors had done all they could for Dykes and that she needed his hospital bed for others. To coin a familiar modern phrase, he was bed blocking.

Cheshire was appalled that there was no provision for someone like Dykes in the National Health Service. He contacted a string of charities and organisations providing support for ex-servicemen on Dykes' behalf, but none would take him. So Cheshire agreed to look after Dykes himself – at the run-down country house.

During the few weeks that Cheshire, with no experience or training, nursed Dykes, word of his altruism spread and following Dykes' death the house, Le Court in rural Hampshire, was filled with a variety of terminally ill people and TB patients. Importantly there were also younger disabled people who though not ill had no provision available and were often stuck in totally unsuitable cottage hospitals or nursing homes for the elderly. Cheshire sought help from family and friends and within months the eponymous charity was formed with a separate management committee drawn from a wide range of contacts. More homes followed and the decision to work principally with disabled people rather than the terminally ill developed directly out of Cheshire's own growing interest in making a difference to the lives of younger people for whom no specialist provision then existed.

As the charity's first volunteer Cheshire was admirably placed to win support and help from others. His charisma was extraordinary and he in turn could inspire people to volunteer their help when they had no intention, initially, of becoming involved. Air Vice Marshall Sir Christopher Foxley-Norris (former chair of The Leonard Cheshire Foundation) reveals that he had absolutely no intention of becoming a trustee yet found himself agreeing after a conversation terminated by Cheshire with the words, ' ... good, well I'm glad that's settled then'.

Another example of the power of Cheshire's presence and personal impact occurred some years later when he was attempting to help Indian colleagues to set up a 'Cheshire Home' near Delhi. A suitable piece of land had been identified but its acquisition was directly against the newly-independent government's policy. Cheshire secured an interview with the Prime Minister, Pandit Nehru, but spent the entire time seemingly tongue-tied. As David Lean the filmmaker, who happened to be with him in India, explains (Morris 2000) Leonard hardly said a word all afternoon. But when the time to leave came, Nehru asked how Cheshire would get back to his hotel. He replied that he'd probably get the bus and then walk. Nehru then did an unheard of thing and summoned his own car and driver to take them back. He waved goodbye and then turned to his aids saying, 'there goes the greatest man I've met since Gandhi. Give him what he wants!'

Founders are often difficult people to work with. They have a vision and are often completely single minded, acting as though they are totally certain of achieving their objectives. They usually inspire employees joining them early in a venture but sometimes frustrate their staff as the organisation grows.

## Moving on from the founder's vision

Organisations and people working within them generally, tend to mimic or at least replicate the behaviour of their leaders – after all that is the model of success so why push water up hill? Yet in not-for-profit and for-profit organisations alike the transition from leadership by the founder to a delegated board with chairs and chief executives can be traumatic and is rarely smooth. In Cheshire's case, he made the transition comparatively easy. His drive to continue exploring new areas and to assist projects around the world meant that he needed (and was able) to allow others to manage. Yet ten years after his death in 1992 the charity still derives inspiration from his vision. In 1975, with characteristic foresight, he made a film called 'thoughts for the future'. This remarkable recording urges trustees, staff and volunteers to go on meeting unmet need and never shirk a decision that needs to be made saying 'Leonard wouldn't have approved'. That was 17 years before he died. Today the charity works as 'Leonard Cheshire' having dropped the Foundation tag to underline the service provision aspects of its work and prevent confusion with grant-making trusts. The organisation itself reports that there are more than 200 projects in 55 countries around the world. In the UK alone up to 5,000 people volunteer on a regular basis, offering help ranging from sitting on local committees to driving, visiting, supporting individuals and, of course, fundraising.

Cheshire's wife, Sue Ryder, was the founder of her own charity which offers palliative care and was, many feel, one of the forerunners of the modern hospice movement. Sadly the transition from her own leadership to that of the board and management was very acrimonious, leading to her resignation and the formation of another charity to pursue her humanitarian objectives called the Bouverie Foundation. Today the Sue Ryder Foundation, operating as Sue Ryder Care, still has the support of thousands of loyal volunteers inspired by Ryder but who continue to work within the organisation still bearing her name. The 400 charity shops have been rebranded to present a consistent message with greater clarity, to both supporters and the public. An awareness campaign during 2001–02 sought to challenge public perceptions about the work of the organisation and the people who use its services in order to underpin that move to greater clarity.

Many organisations experience significant pain in moving from control by the founder to, usually, a more devolved style of management board with professionals exercising their functional skill more strategically. Susan Kay-Williams (2000) has written a fascinating thesis on the various stages of voluntary organisations' fundraising and highlights the important evolutionary steps that effective organisations must negotiate successfully.

# Employees as volunteers

Whilst many in commercial organisations volunteer to work additional hours or attend extra events without pay, they are nevertheless paid members of staff. The motivation for such personal participation might more usually be identified as status enhancement, skill development, team assistance and personal reward by helping the company to perform more effectively. Philanthropy is rarely the motivating force.

However the opportunities to enjoy all of those factors and many more altruistic ones exist when volunteering within the workplace is part of a project to work with not-for-profit organisations. Many good examples exist, from the British Trust for Conservation Volunteers (BTCV) who put together teams of volunteers from corporate participants to work on conservation projects, to Business in the Community (BITC) who are dedicated to encouraging companies to seek out community partners and assist them via employee volunteering schemes. When these are linked with marketing initiatives a much greater synergy can be achieved through shared branding and fundraising activities utilising both staff volunteering input and revenue generation via trading and cause-related marketing. Once again a more integrated approach – from both types of organisation – can result in large increases in added value.

# The changing face of the volunteer

A survey conducted by the *Guardian* (14 september 2002) shows that working for a charity is the top choice amongst men and women. The UK-wide survey conducted amongst 25 to 70-year-old workers revealed an astonishing 22 per cent overall opting to work for a charity if they could shed the shackles of their everyday work. This reveals a fascinating opportunity for charities to provide far more volunteering and secondment opportunities to corporate partners, supporting the government's efforts to promote volunteering and greater participation in and with the voluntary sector. There must surely be creative opportunities for charities to seize, providing innovative volunteering to fit both sets of objectives.

Perhaps what is now needed is not just opportunities for an individual or team to enhance their expertise and people skills but for human resource departments working on staff development programmes to take account of their employees' desires and ambitions. They need to seek creative long-term relationships with not-for-profits where they offer both people and marketing activities so as to raise funds and create additional operational capacity to deliver services. This works whether it is to improve the environment through education campaigns or to enhance the lives of those experiencing discrimination, disaffection and dislocation. Shared values and an increase in public awareness and understanding of such projects could only benefit the commercial and not-for-profit organisations' objectives mutually.

## The beneficiaries

The previous chapter explored the roles of various stakeholders but it is worth considering the *volunteer* role that beneficiaries, in particular, can play for charities and how that differs from the non-monetary contribution customers can make to commercial organisations as part of focus groups or as product champions in return for some purchasing loyalty.

The beneficiaries of the services provided by not-for-profits are rarely customers as such, and their relationship with the service provider is therefore likely to be profoundly different even where the user is not the purchaser (as with the NHS). However, earlier models of grateful, needy clients gaining benefit from a charity's intervention are, not before time, giving way to client consultation, empowerment programmes and active participation in governance by service users. Arthritis Care's board of trustees has moved from having 48 members, few with personal experience of arthritis, to 17 members the majority of whom, including the chair, have the condition. Cancer and disability care charities might consider how they could achieve the same levels of user participation. Trustees are of course not remunerated, so motivation to make a difference, as a volunteer, has to be very high indeed.

## The members

Many not-for-profits are, like Arthritis Care and RNID, membership organisations. In sporting organisations members are usually the principal stakeholders being both the beneficiaries and the funders. Volunteer involvement and marketing challenges however remain much the same as for other not-for-profits.

CASE STUDY **ENGLISH HOCKEY**

English Hockey (formerly The English Hockey Association – EHA) depends upon the affiliation fees from the clubs around the country. Some 60,000 adults continue to play hockey in England and it is considered to be the second most popular team activity (soccer being top). The overwhelming majority of people playing are of course amateur; each affiliated club is run by and for amateurs and these volunteers resent any investment not seen as directly benefiting the game and participating players. Yet the EHA became insolvent because it could not handle the large amounts of funds flowing into the game through grant assistance from Sport UK. Interim chief executive Andrew Hope comments: ' The challenge is to create an infrastructure that can then deliver on facilities, pitches, coaching and player development, whilst being seen by the clubs as relevant and of benefit to them.' He goes on: 'Hockey must be marketed as an exciting, family sport. The integration in

1997 of the men's, women's and mixed sections means we can promote this exciting but non-contact sport to all ages.'

Certainly the sport has moved on since mixed hockey was played by many at college on rough, pitted grass pitches but success in the 1980s when England were World Champions was not translated into club membership, improved facilities or increased corporate support. The infrastructure is being put into place, but can the former success at an international level be repeated?

Without international success how can major corporate support be obtained? Hope continues: 'It's true that money often follows such international success but there are alternatives. Success at a family participation level, and the backing of high profile champions or ambassadors may mean we can interest major brands aimed directly at the family to join with us in growing the sport.'

# Commercial partners

There remains a huge stigma attached to volunteers as amateurs, compared to professionals who are paid and often have impressive qualifications to back their claims of competence and expertise. Conversely, within trustee bodies there is often a dismissive attitude bordering upon contempt for staff and management as 'the hired help' who by definition cannot be as committed as volunteers who give their time for free. Staff, on the other hand, may not think of their trustees as volunteers at all. Sometimes it may be seen almost as a class issue with the board packed by well educated upper-middle-class WASPs (White Anglo Saxon Protestants). This is a debate not usually experienced by the corporate sector; nevertheless, it is highly relevant when it comes to the use of voluntary assistance by the staff of a commercial partner to a charity. These are, it should be remembered, staff who are often highly qualified and experienced in their professional roles. They are people likely to become rapidly demotivated and uninterested unless they feel valued, feel they are making a real contribution and particularly important, are listened to if they make comments and suggestions.

From a marketing perspective the opportunity to use such assistance, whether corporate or individual or from the local community is a wonderful one when it can be properly integrated into the communications plan. Volunteer experiences along with those of service users provide invaluable PR and those same people go on to be long-term champions of the cause espousing their enthusiasm to anyone who will listen. At this level there is real benefit in corporate fundraisers investing significant time and resources into developing friends and supporters within target corporates and those already beginning to work with a charity.

# Trustees

Trustee boards differ in one essential aspect to those boards of directors of for-profit companies: the members are unpaid (though expenses are usually reimbursed). Trustees, like their motivations, come in all shapes and sizes. Many have begun by volunteering with the organisation because they have an affinity with the cause or (more usually) because a friend, colleague or relative asked them to help.

Just as with company directors, trustees have a prime governance and policy role and are legally responsible for the probity of the organisation.

## CASE STUDIES **TRUSTEES**

SL a retired officer became involved at a local level with a national charity through his knowledge and subsequent work in estate agency. Several years of serving successfully on a local committee led to his being approached by an existing trustee with succession planning on his mind. SL accepted a position on the public affairs committee, subsequently became its chair and was invited to join the board of trustees. Whilst charities are increasingly consulting memberships (where they exist) and establishing electoral systems to improve representation within governing structures, the experiences of SL are quite typical of many. Both national charities and the majority of small local not-for-profits often struggle to secure a sufficient quality and quantity of trustees able to operate effectively within the increasingly complex environment of the twenty-first century.

JT a senior manager at BT was on the receiving end of a periodic reorganisation and took early retirement in his fifties. Within six months he had felt the need for the stimulation of work but he had not actively pursued any volunteer links or opportunities. However a former work colleague now with the Prince's Trust recognised that JT's strategic and financial management skills were just waiting to be harnessed. An invitation to a networking event followed and the director of a small student volunteering charity, Student Volunteering UK, made an approach through the mutual friend. At that time the charity was known as SCADU and had a turnover of just £100,000. The volunteer unit at the Home Office were the largest single funder and were concerned about its financial planning; they needed someone with good financial planning skills on the trustee board. JT was interested in the concept, liked the idea of working with younger people and could, critically, understand how his existing skills and talents might be used to help the organisation.

Six years on the charity had repositioned itself, changed its name, was turning over £500,000 and had a growing student support network. Whilst it would be unfair to ascribe all this to the contribution of one trustee, the fact is that the growth and success went hand in glove with a dynamic new director, a revitalised board and clear financial planning.

Significantly JT persuaded the organisation to introduce time limits for length of trustee service. He himself is now faced with succession planning as a new director has been appointed and retirement beckons, although as he says, 'retiring as a trustee doesn't mean I lose interest in the organisation though whether I'll pursue other volunteering roles in this or another organisation remains to be seen.' He has in fact now been taken on as trustee treasurer by MIND, following an open advertisement.

Increasingly not-for-profit organisations are finding it helpful to set time limits on the length of service and many have open elections to ensure that anyone interested in serving has an opportunity to put themselves forward, rather than wait to be asked. One young woman joined the youth section of a national charity dealing with the condition which she had. As an active, committed volunteer she quickly become known to other members and was elected chair of the youth section. With that role came a place on the main trustee board and over time her skills, passion and commitment resulted in her being elected chair of the main charity. She, as an elected chair, is still however very much the exception.

Trustees should be the most committed supporters that a charity has. In the USA trustees are expected to contribute regularly to the cause, not just their time, but financially at whatever level they are able to give. In the UK this is much rarer and service is often seen as an alternative to significant financial support. Yet how many companies would expect to have non-shareholding directors? As referred to in the previous chapter, trustees have a responsibility to understand plans they ask managers to develop and implement and to stand by those plans, reviewing necessary refinements but sticking with strategy once it has been agreed by the organisation.

Marketeers in not-for-profits need to work very closely with their chief executives to gain acceptance and understanding by the entire trustee body of the need to engage with the marketing process and realise the true value locked into the organisation's reputation. In turn trustees have to embrace the changes that this involves and understand that their roles change along with the organisation. This in turn can mean very significant shifts in the types of people becoming trustees and the ways in which they interact.

# Conclusion

As a number of surveys have shown customers and investors show distinct preferences for commercial brands supporting community investment, in line with Ansoff's argument (see p30). This surely is an indicator that many for-profits could improve reputations and public perceptions by participating more fully in community concerns. Moreover through active, well-resourced marketing programmes they could collaborate more productively with appropriate not-for-profits.

Volunteers can be seen to be the UBP (unique benefit proposition) for not-for-profits replacing the USP (unique selling proposition) of the commercial world. Skilled corporate practitioners will make use of both in order to enhance their marketing programmes and develop their brands.

# CHAPTER SEVEN

# Marketing communications – media or message?

'The medium is the message.'                    *Marshall Mcluhan*

'We are coming to the end, the turkey has been
cooked.'                                         *Malcolm McClaren*

This chapter examines the difficulties of communication in the twenty-first century, exploring such issues as media fragmentation and micro audiences. It also explains how the ability to segment, understand key audiences and then target specific groups can benefit marketing campaigns and the marketing plans of companies, charities and community network organisations.

## Perspectives

Mass communication is a relatively new phenomenon. Before improvements in newspaper distribution in the nineteenth century via the railways those wishing to communicate with the population at large (usually the king or his representatives) had to rely on a slow dissemination of information via the written and spoken word through letters, proclamations and the use of town criers. Quite sophisticated systems, based on military signalling – semaphore towers for example – developed to provide emergency point-to-point communications. However individuals wanting to communicate an idea widely had to resort to such methods as 'pamphleteering' which is, of course, still used today by political activists. Addresses from the church pulpit often played an important role in the dissemination of information and influenced how people understood what was going on.

Individual communications were revolutionised first in 1840 with the advent of the penny post and then telegraph communications, which moved from the earlier manual semaphore towers and masts to electrically wired systems. Then in the early twentieth century the availability of the telephone grew to become widespread.

In the later twentieth century the channels open to organisations and individuals wanting to advertise, or communicate a particular message or idea, proliferated rapidly with the advent of radio and television. A very much larger audience was available to UK advertisers from 1958, with the arrival of commercial television. Commercial radio became available relatively late, in 1973, although illegally-operating pirate radio stations offered advertising in the 1960s.

In the 1990s, with the growth of the Internet and electronic mail, the possibilities of mass interactive communications began to exercise organisations keen to reach specific audiences with targeted messages.

Alongside these developments we have seen phenomenal growth in the use of, and power of, computers. One of the most important applications of computing to marketing and particularly, fundraising, has been in the field of direct mail where a single individual or organisation has the ability to 'write' a letter to hundreds, thousands, and now millions of customers or potential clients in an apparently personalised way.

# Direct mail

Historically, direct mail has formed a vital part of nearly all large charity fundraising activities. And even though results, especially to cold mailings aimed at recruiting new donors, continue to decline more players are entering the market as smaller and smaller organisations seek to build regular predictable sources of voluntary income.

## Direct mail statistics

Charity use of direct mail rose by 5 per cent during 2001 with around 266 million items of direct mail being sent to consumers by charities during the year. Fundraising consultant Tony Elischer comments that the 5 per cent increase was predictable. 'If you look at the number of charities coming on stream with direct mailing and the fact that almost everybody recognises the importance of bringing on new recruits, then it's not surprising that the use of direct mail is continuing to rise,' he suggests. 'It's a reflection of the market becoming tougher and charities having to cover all angles.'

Figures from the annual report of the Direct Mail Information Service (DMIS) show that direct mail volumes in general have increased by more than 110 per cent over the past 11 years. The average household in the UK during 2001 received 13 items of direct mail each month, up by half an item compared with 2000. Despite increased use of direct mail by the charity sector, the statistics suggest that only one of these 13 monthly items is likely to be from a charity. They also show that only 43 per cent of consumer direct mail is opened and read, down considerably from the previous year, when the figure was 53 per cent, indicating perhaps that consumer resistance is growing.

Interestingly the annually-produced statistics from the DMIS reveal that the charity sector was responsible for 7.2 per cent of all consumer direct mail by volume in 2001, putting it well ahead of book clubs (3 per cent), travel firms (4 per cent) and utility companies (5.6 per cent). Overall, charities were the fourth biggest users of consumer direct mail, behind the financial sector (35.3 per cent), mail order firms (13.6) and store card providers (9.9).

Like all media, direct mail needs to be used effectively in order to meet the key objectives set out and agreed for it, usually, within the organisation's communications plan. Despite the enormous growth in over the last ten years mail order firms continue to derive the vast majority of their turnover from their mailed catalogue services. The same picture exists for charity trading – traditionally around Christmas gift and card catalogues.

# The Internet

Whilst the British Red Cross, for example, took only a small percentage of their total Christmas 2001 sales via the Internet this was nevertheless a significant increase over the previous year and is certainly expected to continue growing in importance. Jeremy Hughes (previously director of fundraising and now head of resource mobilisation and donor relations for the International Federation of Red Cross and Red Crescent Societies) has a very pragmatic view, however, and comments: 'The Internet is just another way of reaching people. In response to a major international emergency, it is possible to cut through the noise and attract significant funds. Outside of appeals that enjoy such mass media support, the Internet has not yet proved a serious challenger to more traditional direct marketing techniques.'

Fundraisers in charities charged with developing income streams face very similar problems to their sales counterparts in companies.

Investment now has to be spread over an increasingly diverse range of media, including the Internet, as fragmentation gathers pace. The potential of the Internet is perhaps illustrated by growth throughout the 1990s of seasonal charity trading catalogues for spring and sometimes summer both to increase overall sales (or slow their decline) and perhaps more importantly, smooth the resulting trading patterns over more of the year. Online catalogues can be updated at far more regular intervals than their paper counterparts without incurring huge print and distribution costs. Indeed an organisation can be very 'opportunity oriented' listing and de-listing products or services depending upon news and current events. Many Internet portals such as MSN, Virgin, Yahoo and even the BBC respond very quickly to daily or even hourly events posting links and offers that hook directly into people's interest in the event which may, in reality, be quite peripheral. This is covered in more detail in the next chapter.

In the same way as a multimedia approach needs to be applied to mail order and trading, so fundraisers must consider the varying merits of direct mail and E-mail over other channels, depending upon the desired objectives. Clarity is all important and realistic expectations need to temper enthusiasm to get the job done.

Thus, for example, the approach to organising an emergency appeal needs to change quite dramatically from that which may have been successful just five years ago. A fundraising appeal, for an urgent, unexpected activity might then have elicited a 24 per cent response from a database of 220,000 active donors at an average of £21 yielding just over £1.1 million. The costs of that mailing would have been around £110,000 allowing for first class postage and response handling, which would mean a net £1m towards the project. Today's fundraisers, however, would need to organise a multimedia campaign to get anywhere close to these results.

Mail would, probably, still form the backbone of today's appeal. However going to a database of perhaps 250,000 donors would elicit a much lower response rate for two reasons. First, overall response to warm, supporter mailing has dropped significantly over this timeframe and second, most charities have concentrated upon both recruiting new donors via regular giving methods, and converting existing supporters to similar regular donations. The scope therefore for one-off responses to a perceived emergency is much less. The mailing, even with telephone follow-ups, might produce a response of 16 per cent giving an average of £21 (excluding regular monthly donors, averages have changed little over five years) which means a yield of £840,000. However, provided that the organisation has carefully built up E-mail addresses for supporters, enquirers and site visitors, then Internet site announcements and E-mails to all known supporters could easily take the gross back to £1 million if 5 per cent of an E-mail campaign to 100,000 addresses yielded £30 each. The costs overall are however likely to have increased to £150,000 allowing for the differing channel costs and fragmentation. Thus for increased effort and complexity the net contribution may have fallen by £160,000 over the period. (This is a fictitious example but based on a composite of several real examples.)

As Howard Lake, head of Fundraising UK, the leading Internet site for not-for-profit organisations says: 'Times are changing fast. There are charities already making money from Internet only appeals. The E-mail, properly used with the right audiences, can be every bit as effective as a conventional mailed appeal.' Lake continues: 'Amazon remains the benchmark for the application and delivery of good marketing via new media.' He reveals however that some charities are learning fast. Greenpeace are testing online giving using direct debits and Oxfam's online campaigns using microsite technology are enjoying great success. Lake adds: 'Integration of the channels is the big one.' By this he means two things. First, that as marketeers learn to use E-mail and the Internet as an integrated part of their marketing programmes, so the brand values they espouse will be perceived by anyone seeing multiple versions, messages and communications via different media, as coherent and reinforced. Currently many display conflicts between print or television messages and those perceived and interpreted through the Internet. However Lake is also referring to the fact that as television goes digital and the distinction between PC, Internet terminal and TV begins to blur so the need to present coherence will intensify.

Peter Sweatman is founder and chief executive of the Charity Technology Trust (CTT). He believes that the Internet can provide far more than direct marketing opportunities and may be one of the avenues through which corporates and charities can begin to work more closely on joint marketing initiatives, as opposed to collaboration, however worthy, on community affairs and issues. CTT has itself been formed as a charity with the aim of helping other not-for-profits to make much better use of the available technology. Currently CTT has 25 partners who use a common platform to provide online ticket sales and promotional opportunities for charity lotteries. This uniquely allows participating organisations to have an online dimension to an existing lottery so that there is no need to secure additional prizes or ticket distribution. Sweatman explains, 'the cost of developing a bug free, secure platform would be prohibitive for any individual charity. We provide a single platform with multiple use and already have raised £70 k extra revenue for our partners'. He goes further: 'However this is only the start. The lottery engine is a practical, valuable example of what we can deliver because we have the knowledge, expertise and backing to continue investing and developing other platforms. CTT needs to be considered as the single source for such technology. Ultimately our boiler plates should be free.' By this he means CTTs products will be like other software: first generation products are expensive, the next generation are produced in volume and more cheaply and finally programs and utilities become shareware. This is how he envisages CTT being able to grow and service the needs of many more not-for-profits.

# Mobile phones

Not-for-profits are, of course, always looking for new ways to raise money quickly and easily and many are turning to the boom in mobile phone technology to boost donations. Text messaging – SMS (small messaging service) – is already being used to carry broadcast advertising by both network operators and mainstream advertisers seeking to influence the predominantly younger audiences using the technology.

Comic Relief asked people to sign up to receive messages in the run-up to Sport Relief day in July 2002 and raised 1 per cent of their £10 million total by SMS. It ran two competitions and 320,000 supporters text messaged or phoned their answers to a premium rate number costing £1, of which 60p went to the charity. 'It was a big success,' says Jackie White, media relations manager for Comic Relief. 'This was the first time a UK charity had used SMS to fundraise but we are definitely planning to do it again on Red Nose Day next March. It's a very easy way for people to get involved.'

CASE STUDY **CAFOD**

A charity which is already exploiting the popularity of text messaging is the international overseas development agency Cafod. It plans to run disaster appeals by using text messages to encourage spontaneous giving when global crises are reported. The charity has been experimenting with the technology for a year and believes it offers a good way to get a rapid response. For example a disaster report on the 10 o'clock news could be followed by a bleep on existing supporters' mobile phones, signalling a text message from Cafod asking them to pledge money. People could then text back the amount they wish to donate, and it could be deducted from their bank or credit card where an existing mandate or authority already exists. 'This would give us instant access to our supporters and mean we could act much more quickly to raise emergency aid,' says Nick Buxton, Cafod's web development manager. 'We are negotiating with phone operators and hope to have the scheme up and running next year.' Charities have only recently begun to exploit the potential benefits of text messaging but already results are impressive.

Cafod feels that it is not yet big enough to run an appeal similar to that of Comic Relief because using a premium rate line donors only give 60 p at a time. However, under Cafod's planned scheme – where donors can make far larger pledges – the money raised would cover the expense of employing the necessary technical and processing staff and prove more cost effective. One big advantage of SMS is that it allows charities to reach much younger audiences than those of existing donor groups. Cafod runs competitions and sends out messages to teenagers who opt into their fast-track SMS service and supporters can also download Cafod logos onto their mobile phones. 'We want people to feel like a community, that they are involved, rather than just associating the charity with appeals for money,' Buxton adds. It's not just teenagers who like texting either. Over 45 million text messages are sent in the UK every day, according to the Mobile Data Association, and reaching adults by SMS has also proved beneficial.

Cafod set up a text messaging service for the Trade Justice Movement (TJM) lobby, which it supported, in June 2002 succeeding in signing up 1,100 people – almost 10 per cent of the 12,000 who went to Westminster to lobby their MPs for fairer international trade (see p124).

Brand2Hand, the company who organised the mechanics of the text messaging campaign for TJM, are now working on emerging technologies to help charities, such as picture messaging or MMS (multimedia messaging device being offered in third generation phones). 'But the single biggest thing that is coming in the future is the wider spread of the existing technologies,' said Brand2Hand director, Richard Lander. 'Most charities haven't even caught up with that. For instance charities can contact their supporters by geographical area via SMS, so telling all the supporters in the northwest if there's an event coming up in Manchester.'

Another area ripe for development is wireless connection. Palmtop computers are now starting to have phone functions as well as wireless Internet connections through which users can link together in a 'mesh' and communicate with each other. Such chat forums are already being used by community groups in London and Devon. Cafod is also exploring the idea, which would allow its supporters to talk to each other and swap fundraising tips. 'The crucial thing is that the technology is already available and it's cheaper than having to go out and buy a new 3G phone,' comments Lander.

But text messaging and new technology are unlikely to replace other forms of campaigning. Jenny Walters, policy officer of the Institute of Fundraising, said SMS is likely to remain one of a package of techniques, like direct mail. 'The great thing is that wherever people go they take their mobile so charities can reach them immediately, rather than having to wait for them to go into work to look at their E-mails,' she said. 'But there is only space to get across a short message using mobile phones, so there will still be a need for in-depth leaflets and the like.'

If all else fails it is possible to make money from unwanted and redundant mobiles, like used toner and obsolete computers before them. ChildLine and other not-for-profits have launched schemes to recycle such equipment, gaining up to £30 per handset, for use in the developing world.

# Print media

For many years newspaper and magazine advertising has been the staple recruitment medium for charities and many commercial organisations. Stephen Pidgeon, chairman of sector agency Target Direct says: 'Print is still alive and well.' To Pidgeon's mind however what has altered is the rate of change. He feels that with direct marketing budgets for print and mail being cut in favour of face-to-face recruitment charities, agencies are having to work harder, faster and 'smarter' to achieve acceptable results.

Pidgeon points to the umbrella campaign 'Remember a Charity'. This has been launched by the Legacy Campaign, which is working on behalf of nearly 100 charities, to raise awareness of the benefits of writing a favourite cause into your will. It aims over time to help increase the percentage of those writing charitable bequests into their wills from just over 13 per cent to 15 per cent – not a huge increase but capable, if successful of raising an additional £2 billion for good causes. The hidden face of the campaign is working to influence financial advisers and will-makers to be much more upfront in asking clients whether they want to help a favourite cause in this way. An example of the campaign is featured (see Figure 13), alongside a more conventional charity will advertisement (see Figure 14). It remains to be seen whether such a campaign, distanced from the very powerful causes it espouses to help, can make any real difference.

**FIGURE 13** EXAMPLE OF AN ADVERTISEMENT FROM THE 'REMEMBER A CHARITY' CAMPAIGN

# Don't let our good work stop when you die

Charities that help or rescue people in times of danger and crisis depend on the kind generosity of supporters like you. Whether you give money or time, your help plays a vital part in their life-changing work.

So isn't it good to know you can go on helping your favourite charity long into the future, simply by including them in your will? The donation will be tax-free and you can leave as much or as little as you want.

Talk to your solicitor about leaving money to the causes you are passionate about.

Or for a free information pack explaining how to put your favourite charity in your will, you can also telephone **0808 1 80 20 80,** (minicom 0808 1 80 80 30) or visit our website **www.rememberacharity.org.uk**.

**everyone can leave the world a better place**
remember a charity in your will

**Charities working together for a better future**

Registered Charity Number 1079573

**FIGURE 14** EXAMPLE OF A 'LEGACY' ADVERTISEMENT

### BROOKE HOSPITAL FOR ANIMALS
*founded in 1934 by Dorothy Brooke*

# Your legacy will bring good fortune...

...to a hard-working brick kiln donkey in India,
or an ill-treated horse in Egypt.

For almost 70 years, the Brooke Hospital
has been changing lives in the world's
poorest countries. We ease the suffering of
sick and injured working horses, donkeys
and mules with free veterinary treatment.
And we show their owners how good
animal management can benefit them, too.

Our work is enduring, reaching generation after
generation of animal owners. With your support,
we can work together to make a real difference
– for years to come.

So when you are remembering friends and family in your
Will, please consider remembering the Brooke Hospital.
You will bring lasting good fortune to animals in need.

**Brooke Hospital for Animals, Broadmead House
21 Panton Street, London SW1Y 4DR.**
**Registered Charity No. 1085760**

To speak to our Legacy Manager, please call
**020 7968 0807**
or email: **legacies@brooke-hospital.org.uk**
for advice or further information.

Your legacy won't just help treat the pain of
overworked donkeys like Basanthi here. It will ensure
that her owner knows how to respect and care for the
animal he depends on – and his children will, too.

# Broadcast media

John Logie Baird demonstrated the first television broadcast in 1924 and the BBC made the first public broadcasts (using EMI's rival electronic version) in 1936. However it was not until the Coronation in 1953 that TV set ownership took off in the UK and began a communications revolution still going on today. In 1958 the first commercial television station opened with an advertisement for Gibbs SR toothpaste and for many years the cost and perceived value of broadcast TV advertising dictated that well established consumer brands were the only regular users of the media.

Radio and television are the mainstays of much FMCG advertising and many larger charities have invested, with varying levels of success, in the use of such media for direct response advertisements to recruit new donors. What has changed over the last few years is the increasing rate of fragmentation of channels and programming. This means that achieving the task of showing the right advertisement at the right time to the right audience is proving ever more difficult to achieve.

Interactive television has for some time held out the possibility of engaging with the right audience and securing not just orders or donations, but an informed response and feedback to issues and campaigns presented. Unfortunately in the UK this had been, until the demise of ITV digital and the launch of the BBC/Sky competitive response, the bailiwick of the satellite and cable operators with, proportionately, very small audiences. Five 'free to view' channels have now become 35 and the potential to build upon this is enormous.

In addition the Internet, with its increasing ability to carry broadband video communications into the home, and the cinema with an ever increasing number of multiplex, small screen operations offer additional outlets for sponsored and supported programming by not-for-profits even if direct advertising remains beyond them on cost grounds. In reality, with small audiences and even more specialist programming, appealing to limited constituencies, advertising and sponsorship rates will fall further in real terms offering opportunities to quite small organisations. However to contact these small audiences effectively through mobile communications, the Internet, interactive TV, cinema and video or DVD, the organisation must seek each individual's explicit permission.

As Phil Nunn at Optimedia, one of the larger media-buying organisations says: 'The challenge is to see how this fragmentation can be capitalised upon. Advertisers who can learn to use permission marketing will lead the way.' Nunn's view is that a more holistic approach will have to evolve because the new generation of consumers not only 'want it now' but also want it more easily and more simply. Audience fragmentation is then, like so many things, both a threat and an opportunity.

# Conveying the right message to the right audience

Marketing communications, increasingly referred to as Marcoms, is all about getting the right messages to the right audiences. Yet however good the intentions, implementation can produce unexpected and sometimes undesired results.

When Gordon Brown as chancellor made sweeping changes to the tax regime surrounding charitable gifts in his 2002 budget he could hardly have dreamt that at times his generosity would come back to haunt him. The major changes to Gift Aid are being communicated by charities to their supporters and to the well disposed via the Giving Campaign (set up to promote greater philanthropy and tax efficient giving as an NCVO initiative and chaired by Lord Joffe). The campaign is working on a number of fronts but has already rebranded Gift Aid, given it a logo and a much more public face. Increasing numbers of charitable donors now automatically Gift Aid their donations. According to the Inland Revenue £2 billion was given in Gift Aid in the 2001/2 tax year. The right message had reached the right audience.

However the double taxation benefit enjoyed by the donor when making a gift of shares to a charity can be used in distinctly less than philanthropic ways. The intention is to allow any donor to make a gift of shares and enjoy both the tax relief on the gift as well as a write off of any taxable capital gain.

The *Independent* (25 October 2002) reported that an entrepreneur saved £112,000 in tax by donating shares to a charity when they were suspended pending a deal. The entrepreneur gave £280,000 worth of Knutsford shares to the British Wheelchair Sports Foundation. At the time of the transfer the shares were worth 80p but they later collapsed when trading resumed. The charity still holds the shares which are now worth just over £9,000. The tax benefit was secured under the terms of the gift of shares scheme, introduced at the peak of the stock market boom. This share transfer was legal but might put pressure on the government to tighten up the rules on charitable share giving.

More positively, it may be that donating shares to charity could be popular among venture entrepreneurs. Selling shares could damage investor sentiment in their companies. Donating to a charity would lock in an immediate tax benefit on shares which are highly valued at the time. Also, many entrepreneurs are subject to 'lock-in' arrangements, which bar them from selling shares within a year of their stock market float. But, depending on the wording of the flotation prospectuses, the lock-ins may not cover share donations.

Many have of course taken advantage of the new scheme in a genuinely philanthropic way. For example the chairman of microchip designer Arm Holdings donated Arm shares worth £500,000 to the University of Liverpool. In addition the founder of the software company Autonomy, plans to give some £300,000 of Autonomy shares to Christ's College, Cambridge. These moves entitle the donors to an income tax benefit but also help them to avoid the capital gains tax that would be payable if the shares were simply sold and cash given to the charities instead.

# The changing face of communication and communicator

The proliferation of television channels, programming and as a consequence the emergence of micro audiences is a challenge that marketeers of all persuasions ignore at their peril. Phil Nunn of Optimedia gives a useful example of how a not-for-profit might react. 'The RNLI might, in seeking to promote their own extension of work from solely traditional off-shore work to include high speed inshore inflatables working in estuaries, attempt to appeal to a much younger audience for this new market segment.' He suggests that using permission marketing, capturing enquiries from young Internet surfers, text messages via mobiles and short video clips via Internet portals could focus on real life adventures, experiences and shared feelings. The overlap with traditional donors, who respond to direct mail, press and TV advertisements, would be almost zero and the risk therefore of cannibalisation or confusion would be minimised, while the opportunity to engage new young audiences could be extremely fruitful.

This ability to think about audience segmentation is, or should be, already at the heart of donor and customer communications programmes. As referred to in Chapter two segmentation (if only on the lines of donation history: recency, frequency and monetary value) can be taken much further and can be a very good indicator of future behaviour for supporter prospects. Equally the type of operation and style of communication that an organisation exhibits can affect the way in which it is perceived by its target audiences.

## Social enterprises

Social enterprises, referred to in Chapter one, can cut across conventional boundaries, challenging stereotypes and enabling the participants to achieve what others would regard as impossible. They are usually hybrid organisations formed as a direct response to unmet need where conventional structures (public, private and voluntary) have failed to overcome the often huge obstacles standing in the way of improvements, social action and change. They are able to involve audiences seemingly impossible to communicate with – yet once involved these target groups can become not only fully engaged but also active participants in the enterprise itself. Social change is usually a strong motivating force but, in contrast to charity work, individual profit can also be actively encouraged. Anthony Mawson, speaking at the 2002 CAF Conference had some revealing things to say. He considers that charity is not necessarily a good thing, because it can create a dependency culture in the sector with projects endlessly awaiting their next public sector grant. He feels that this dependency can dampen an entrepreneurial spirit, encouraging projects to operate 'in the box' of one funding stream rather than to look 'out of the box' for integrated solutions to social problems. Mawson agrees with Liam Black, chief executive of the Furniture Resource Centre – a social enterprise in Liverpool – who argues that many in the voluntary sector need weaning off charity and grants in favour of a business response to social problems.

This is coincidentally the aim of the community action network (CAN), a social enterprise of which Mawson is an executive director. CAN is a mutual support service for social entrepreneurs working across the UK and is seeking to move traditional charitable projects away from a culture of dependency towards becoming more sustainable social enterprises, where an increasing proportion of the organisation's income comes through trading. He acknowledges that this is easier to do when making furniture or removing bulky waste products, and more complicated when you get into the area of delivering community care and health services in areas where there is little surplus income.

Mawson comments that he has seen millions of pounds of charitable monies wasted in charities: that too many people possess too much ideology and too little know-how about using money in a business-like way. He suggests a collaborative way forward that might retain and promote the energy required to communicate and act where both conventional for-profit and not-for-profits would wilt. Mawson thinks it might be time to create something like an Ofsted for the voluntary sector; a team of experienced business and social entrepreneurs would go in and look at how charities are using their hard-earned cash and mark them appropriately on their ability to deliver services. However, unlike Ofsted, it would need to be entrepreneurial in inspiration, assessing the people and the projects rather than their paperwork, and rewarding risk-taking. It might also act as a receiver, shutting down ineffective organisations and selling on their projects, ideas, and people where they have value. This team could then encourage smaller projects to stop competing and band together, turning their islands of operation into continents of high quality action. Those projects that continue to hold out as islands, refusing to use their assets in favour of the community, would be closed down. Mawson acknowledges that this approach sounds harsh but he is adamant that in some inner-city estates existing charities (including the churches) are in fact creating a culture that perpetuates the conditions they seek to change.

This point of view takes us way beyond even the recommendations of the government's own strategy unit in terms of changes and regulation for charities. However, as discussed in Chapter nine, change and evolution over time is inevitable.

# Doing things differently
## Maintaining a coherent message

Whilst, as Oxfam illustrates, a comprehensive approach to marketing is not impossible, it remains very rare. Simon Collings, ex director of fundraising, agrees that the charity is planning a complete review of the organisation's marketing, which could take it through to 2005 before restructuring and the resulting improvements are completed. Collings says, 'we're making these changes to put the supporter, not the campaign, at the heart of all our communications and fundraising activity'. This is music to the ears of those who firmly believe not-for-profits must take a holistic approach to marketing and ensure that donors, customers and clients receive coherent, welcome messages from the organisation that they have chosen to support or trade with. Oxfam has already gone a long way down the route of marketing coherence but, as Collings says, 'like a lot of modern businesses, we're turning away from promoting a range of products and are beginning to ask ourselves how people want to interact with the Oxfam brand'. He adds: 'The crucial element is changing the way people work, to get them thinking beyond the particular operational role they may have and seeing how this fits into the overall strategy of the organisation.' He concludes that: 'Many staff working for charities don't have marketing backgrounds. We have to ensure staff have a good understanding of supporters and what they are looking for. We also need staff to be constantly making connections with the work of colleagues and looking for opportunities to inspire supporters. This requires a different type of leadership from senior managers who have to act more as creative catalysts and less as traditional managers. Without a change to the internal culture it will be very difficult to achieve our goals.'

## Maintaining a consistent message

Tony Cram (2001) cites the example of Flora, produced by Unilever subsidiary Van den Bergh Foods. The brand values relate to caring, health and trust and the brand conveys a professional approach to healthy living. Every brand encounter confirms the message. From the first advertisements in 1965 'Flora puts natural goodness into good eating' to the message in 2000 'Flora people care' the brand has communicated a consistent core theme. The ongoing sponsorship of the London marathon is totally consistent with the product's healthy identity and the way that the sponsorship is executed each year follows precisely the brand standards. Further promotion with the British Heart Foundation follows similar consistent lines. Pack design is clear, bright and lively and packs carry a care-line telephone number. Call this number and the agents taking the calls are brand champions. They sound professional, helpful and have a high level of expert knowledge. Similarly the website is a valuable source of health information and consistent images. To the best practitioners every point of contact with the brand must be in keeping with the expectations set.

## Reinforcing brand values

Cram's main argument in his book *Customers that Count* (2001) is that organisations must learn to value their best customers and supporters. He reminds us of the old 80/20 rule, the Pareto principle that repeatedly demonstrates that 80 per cent of business is done by 20 per cent of the customers or, more usually, 20 per cent of clients help generate 80 per cent of the profit. Commercial and not-for-profit organisations have to work very hard to ensure those 20 per cent in particular have a special relationship with the organisation. As Flora shows, appropriate investment in working with not-for-profits can be very necessary to reinforce and maintain brand values.

Yet some of the portents for charities are not good. During 2001 large companies donated less of their profits to charity, reducing their level of giving for the first time in six years, according to published figures from DSC (the Directory of Social Change). The top 400 UK companies gave £499 million in total contributions including £286 million in cash donations in 2000–01, a total of 0.44 per cent of pre-tax profits, 0.2 per cent less than the previous year. Charity sector analyst DSC, which compiled the report, said: 'Although we are now seeing the first decrease since 1994–95, it is far too early to know whether this is a blip or the emergence of a serious downward trend.'

## Promoting corporate giving

Levels of UK company giving are in stark contrast to the USA, where there are more tax incentives to give to charity. There, corporate donations to charities average 1 per cent of pre-tax company profits, nearly five times more than that of companies in the UK, and this is despite much publicity calling for companies to give more. A *Guardian* survey of company giving (2001) was described as 'a wake up call' by the Confederation of British Industry.

The Directory of Social Change (Smyth 2002) estimates that companies have the 'capacity if not the will' to put more back into society. It estimates that if every company it surveyed donated 1 per cent of total profits to charity, around £1.2 billion would flow to good causes every year. Among the notable misers were oil giant BP, which only gave 0.09 per cent of pre-tax profits, whilst financial services company HSBC Holdings donated only 0.07 per cent of pre-tax profits. Supermarket retailer Tesco, despite its high profile donations to schools (which has earned it huge amounts of positive media coverage and public approval) only gave 0.16 per cent of pre-tax profits.

Not surprisingly, Lloyds TSB topped the table for the second year, giving £40 million in total contributions, including cash, employees volunteering time and 'in-kind' donations. This equates to 1.03 per cent of pre-tax profits, and owes much to the original set up of the TSB foundations which in turn benefited from the merger with Lloyds. The vast majority of Britain's 3.7 million businesses do not donate anything at all to charity; 99 per cent of donations are accounted for by the top 400 companies and the top 25 account for nearly 50 per cent of the total contributions.

However, not all measures of corporate contributions show such a bleak picture. Business in the Community's (BITC) Per Cent Club, which was set up to enable companies to demonstrate the totality of social investment, including cash, employees' time, skills and resources, has shown a 50 per cent increase in investment over the last four years to 2001. Peter Davies, deputy chief executive of Business in the Community, has stated that: 'Donations to the community are only one aspect of corporate responsibility. Business in the Community encourages its members to focus on issues in the workplace, marketplace and environment, as well as in the community.'

The challenge then is to find the different ways for commercial and not-for-profits to work more closely, following the examples of corporates such as HSBC and Tesco who are beginning to understand the long-term value of effective partnerships.

# Conclusion

As Marshall Mcluhan is quoted as saying at the beginning of this chapter, the medium is the message but marketeers now have the opportunity to select the media and the message. A mismatch inevitably results in brand confusion, loss of consumer confidence and reduced supporter participation. Congruence leads to increased synergy, a growing reputation and the inspiration of confidence in all participants. Where the organisation cannot adapt, or does not have the right fit, it must take on appropriate partners. That is the marketing challenge.

# CHAPTER EIGHT

# Reaching your audiences

'Never walk away from failure. On the contrary study it for its hidden assets.'

*Michael Korda*

'When choosing between two evils I like to try the one I've never tried before.'

*Mae West*

The previous chapter looked at the difficulty of communicating via ever fragmenting channels. This chapter examines more closely the various communications methods that are available to marketeers, together with the issues that surround them. It includes a discussion on the use of shock tactics in advertising and the need for real life stories in the media. Specific use of the Internet and other new media is also examined and contrasted, and the abiding power of passion is commented upon.

## Perspectives

The fragmentation that has occurred in print, broadcast media and through the Internet over the last decade presents both dangers and opportunities for those seeking to communicate key messages, establish brand identities and elicit support either through sales or donations.

Mobile phone technology has assisted in the proliferation of communications channels with text messaging, WAP and SMS providing further opportunities to reach highly segmented target audiences. The technology already exists, should the organisations choose to use them, not just for McDonalds to text customers nearing branches about special offers, but for Oxfam to text potential customers approaching one of their 850 retail outlets in the UK.

With DRTV it has become far more affordable for small- to medium-sized not-for-profits to mount a campaign aimed at key target audiences via the large number of cable and satellite channels. Whilst audiences may not be large it might well become possible to purchase airtime dependent upon response rates.

The growth in local FM radio stations has fragmented radio audiences further (and increased competition for the advertisers' budgets) making it even harder to buy media simply by audience figures and demographics alone. Instead, to be effective, media buyers have to consider the acceptability to the audience of a particular message, and the context in which that message will be received.

For not-for-profits, using direct mail to recruit new donors and elicit continuing funds from existing donors, the problem is much the same. As the volumes of cold mail grow, existing donors known to be DM responsive become increasingly alienated by charity communications and so responses to cold and warm mailings fall inexorably. The challenge is for the communicating organisation to create context and greater relevance.

# Shock tactics

Such tactics are used in campaigns seeking to grab an audience's attention by mobilising outrage. Amnesty International UK has made use of photographs of horrendous instruments of torture, alongside the stories of the victims of such devices. Although it has recently begun to move away from such deliberately shocking images in its press campaigns, Amnesty International has had some success in the past with advertisements such as this one, shown in Figure 15.

## FIGURE 15 EXAMPLE OF THE USE OF 'SHOCK' ADVERTISING

# The police had a trick that left little Alfonso speechless.

**The Brazilian police know exactly how to keep street children quiet – pull or cut out their tongues.**

Corpses bearing the gruesome signs of torture – eyes burned from their sockets, ears and tongues sliced off – are turning up with horrifying regularity on the streets of Brazil.

Amnesty International has evidence of torture in over 125 countries. It's hard to imagine, but right now, thousands of people are suffering for their beliefs or the colour of their skin.

By supporting Amnesty International, you can help bring an end to the horror – and bring the culprits to justice. Please spare a moment to return this coupon or call the number below. If you knew the difference it would make, you wouldn't think twice.

## Help us cut out torture
# 0845 601 2060

## Yes, I want to support Amnesty International

UK residents only, please send the completed form to:
Amnesty International, FREEPOST, London EC1B 1HE.

Name: (Mr/Mrs/Miss/Ms)

Address:

Postcode:

### I want to become a member

☐ Individual £24    ☐ Family £30    ☐ Youth (under 22) £7.50

☐ Senior Citizen £7.50   ☐ Student £7.50    ☐ Claimant £7.50

As a member of Amnesty International UK, you'll receive our bi-monthly magazine that gives information on human rights abuse around the world, and how you can help.

### And/or I want to give a donation

I wish to make a donation towards Amnesty International's vital work

£250 ☐    £100 ☐    £50 ☐    £25 ☐    £other ☐

Please make cheque/po payable to Amnesty International UK, or enter your Visa or Mastercard number below (we do not accept Switch)

☐☐☐☐ ☐☐☐☐ ☐☐☐☐ ☐☐☐☐

Valid from ☐☐ ☐☐    Expiry date ☐☐ ☐☐

Signed

If you are making a gift by credit card, please attach your credit card billing address if different from above.
Amnesty International sends its members information about sympathetic organisations. If you do not want to receive these mailings please tick. ☐

**AMNESTY INTERNATIONAL** UNITED KINGDOM

AT111

Amnesty's current advertising shocks the reader by comparing the ease with which UK readers can join the organisation with the difficulties experienced by Amnesty International members elsewhere in the world.

## Appropriateness and relevance

It is vital that the appropriateness of anything that may shock is given thorough consideration very early in the planning of any such campaign, and that all the ramifications are worked through, to gain the agreement of all those who may have to respond to criticism and comment. The organisation must be fully aware of the possible impact and how to counter both press comment and individual criticism. Action plans need to be produced, likely question and answer scenarios developed and perhaps most important of all, internal communications must ensure that the whole organisation knows why such tactics are being used within a campaign or strategy.

In the development of donor relationships many fundraisers are increasingly moving away from negative imagery which may produce a short-term guilt reaction with an uplift in donations but which has the danger to alienate long-term supporters who become weary of having, as they might feel, their emotions manipulated. Arthritis Care developed a set of guidelines around the question: 'Is it – POSITIVE, HONEST, POWERFUL and URGENT?' with regard to fundraising and awareness advertising to avoid criticisms by people with arthritis of being turned into victims, sufferers and as a result of the demeaning stereotypes, incompetent people deserving only pity. By concentrating on positive outcomes the charity was able to square the circle around capturing attention, interest, desire and action without alienating service users. For campaigns aimed at mobilising awareness and action, say, from government the organisation used 'outrage' and the sense of injustice about issues of lack of facilities or resources for the 8 million people with arthritis in the UK today. This integrated well with the fundraising strategy and enabled each to work off the other.

The use of shock must be equally carefully considered in relation to existing donors, making sure that they are aware, for example, that a campaign is about to break, why the organisation is using particular tactics, the expected outcomes and what (if anything) is expected of them. This can go a very long way towards preventing criticism and a negative response arising from important segments of the very audience that has been targeted.

## CASE STUDY BARNARDO'S

From 2001–03 Barnardo's shocked the public by running explicit advertisements portraying the victims of child abuse and depravation and the impact upon the child's later life in terms of suicide, prostitution and drug abuse. Barnardo's deny that the campaign ('Stolen childhood') was designed to shock readers gratuitously but agree they do want people to reappraise their attitudes both to Barnardo's – the organisation – and to the issues about which they campaign and provide services.

Their series featured adult faces superimposed upon the bodies of children with the strapline 'Abuse through prostitution steals children's lives.' and it caused complaints to the Advertising Standards Authority. A spokeswoman for the ASA said: 'People have found the adverts distressing, offensive and unsuitable to be seen by children.' Barnardo's responded that: 'We wanted to make an impact ... but we are not in the arena of shock advertising.' Barnardo's previously courted controversy by running an awareness campaign using a similar age manipulation device; one advertisement showed a baby injecting heroin.

The technology may now be more sophisticated but these campaigns are in fact only the latest in a tradition established in the nineteenth century by the founder, Thomas John Barnardo (1845–1905). After his first homes for orphans began to open in the 1870s, Barnardo used photographs of his rescued children in advertisements for fundraising – a skill of which he was master. 'Before' and 'after' pictures would be taken, showing orphans in a state of neglect on rescue from the street, and afterwards, all scrubbed clean and full of promise. But in 1877 Barnardo found himself accused of artificially staging the photographs, alongside other allegations that he enriched himself with charity money and that children were physically abused in his homes. Some of Barnardo's accusers felt the images were indecent and provocative in displaying the bare limbs and bodies of the children. One can only imagine what they would have made of the current, overtly sexualised campaign.

George Reynolds, an evangelical Baptist minister, denounced Barnardo's staging of the photographs as destroying the 'better feelings' of the children. In July 1877, Barnardo admitted in court the artistic license he took with the photography, claiming that he never intended to make particular portraits but rather wanted to depict individuals as representative of their 'class'. His defence to the court is a classic in the history of back-footed rhetoric and is worth quoting:

' ... we are often compelled to seize the most favourable opportunities of fine weather, and the reception of some boy or girl of a less destitute class whose expression of face, form, and general carriage may, if aided by suitable additions or subtractions of clothing convey a truthful picture of the class of children received in unfavourable weather, whom we could not photograph immediately'.

Barnardo was cleared of most charges and *The Times* assured the public that his homes were 'real and valuable charities, worthy of public confidence and support'. However there was condemnation of his methods, which the court said were not only 'morally wrong ... but might, in the absence of very strict control, grow into a system of deception dangerous to the cause on behalf of which it is practised'. The case was particularly significant because the status of photography was, at that time, a medium by which some kind of visual 'truth' was supposed to be revealed. The idea that Barnardo had staged many of his photographs destabilised the Victorians' notion of authenticity. A deliberately manipulated photograph of a child was considered not just an assault on notions of representational truth, but an assault on the innocence of the child itself.

Today such hand-wringing about the authenticity of images is less marked in a society where the public is much more aware of the sleights of hand that manipulate visual culture. Steve Hilton, a partner of prominent social marketing agency Good Business, maintains that manipulating imagery in the current 'Stolen childhood' campaign is legitimate, and that it was not a bad thing for Dr Barnardo to have done it in the 1870s. 'That's no longer an interesting debate. What I am interested in is how effectively campaigns are in fulfilling their objectives. It is not enough just to raise awareness, they have to achieve a tangible social benefit,' he comments. Indeed, if Barnardo could see how his charity is now manipulating children's images, similarly for ultimately defendable good works, he might well feel vindicated. Clearly it was not just in matters of philanthropy, but also in marketing, that he was a maverick and a visionary.

# Advertising versus editorial

It is in the area of 'free' editorial, the comment and reportage on such 'shock' campaigns, that their value probably lies. It is often said that editorial coverage is worth several times the value of the equivalent area of advertising. But this is only true if the message is translated effectively and names or brand identities are as clearly identifiable as they would be in the equivalent advertisement. It is true that a quarter-page editorial is likely to be read by far more of the prospective audience than an equivalent advertisement but again unless there is clarity all the effort may, in awareness terms, be wasted.

The difficulty lies, of course, in ensuring that the message, including important identity tags such as names, logos and brand marks is transmitted through the journalist's desire to make the story interesting, relevant and objective for their target audiences.

An effective example of the use of editorial comment was the Greenpeace campaign against Esso's plans to dump the North Sea oilrig *Brent Spar* at the bottom of a Norwegian Fjord, which utilised strong shock reaction in its audience. Even though Greenpeace's technical arguments in favour of dismantling, storing and reprocessing were open to question, the organisation overwhelmingly won the PR debate, forcing Esso to reappraise the entire disposal programme.

# Real stories – real people

Journalists always want to hear about real people; after all, real people read their reports. For any campaign, suitable case studies of people willing and able to be interviewed must be prepared. All too often press releases are prepared with suitable quotations but insufficient preparation to ensure anyone likely to comment 'live' is able to talk fluently about the issues including all aspects of branding that need to be communicated. Often the only way to ensure that photographs capture the essence of branding is to use over-printed t-shirts, sweatshirts, banners and other display materials against which people pose or speak. These simple techniques are all too often overlooked in attempts to keep reporters and photographers happy. Against this has to be weighed the dangers of exploitation: adopting a 'triumph over tragedy' or 'victims in adversity' angle, where simplistic stereotyping demeans or worse, detracts from the true story.

Leonard Cheshire's Enabled campaign aims to persuade more mainstream corporate advertisers to use disabled models in their advertising, not because of or in spite of the fact that they are disabled, but simply because disabled people make up nearly 1 in 7 of the population and are therefore 'a slice of life'. They also happen to make up nearly 15 per cent of most consumer advertisers' markets. Part of the campaign is a modelling competition directed at younger disabled people who are keen to become models; this is designed to counter agency and advertiser claims that there are 'no suitable disabled models.' This part of the campaign has been enormously successful in gaining media attention because of the human interest stories. Four minutes on the BBC's evening news and a two-page feature in the *London Evening Standard* are a tribute to the work of the charity's media team.

However whilst the Enabled campaign, and its messages, was well reported, the charity's ownership and organisation of the campaign received virtually no coverage. Does this matter if it helps the campaign achieve its objectives? In absolute terms possibly not since it could be argued that the campaign is, in effect, the brand. However within the organisation's overall communications plan is the express objective to challenge public perceptions of the work the organisation does and help it appeal to a younger audience. Therefore it could be argued that that news and feature coverage was a missed opportunity. Clearly what the charity should have done was to piggy back on the excellent reportage and to augment that coverage by tactical advertising in the corporate and specialist marketing media, together perhaps with further referrals via direct marketing materials or offers.

# Budgetary considerations

For not-for-profit organisations, budget is often a further strongly motivating factor. For a team of two working with a tiny budget the Trade Justice Movement (TJM) achieved a remarkable success. In 2002 it not only organised one of the biggest mass lobbies of parliament in history but a survey of MPs revealed that the campaign had had real impact. The TJM's campaign for fairer international trade was judged the most effective in the biannual charity awareness survey by nfpSynergy, part of the Future Foundation. The RNID and the NSPCC with much larger budgets were beaten into second and third place.

---

**CASE STUDY   TRADE JUSTICE MOVEMENT (TJM)**

The TJM was formed two years ago after Oxfam, Friends of the Earth and 40 other voluntary groups saw the success of the coalition Jubilee 2000 campaign on world debt and realised they would be more effective campaigning together for fair trade.

Last winter plans were formed for a mass lobby of MPs who, it was felt, were not aware of the strength of feeling about fair trade among their constituents. The secret of the campaign's success lies in thorough planning and the combined clout it was able to wield, steering a broad coalition. Ms Holt the TJM's coordinator commented: 'The crucial time was the five months leading up to the lobby. All the charities in the coalition mobilised their members, asking them to write to their MPs requesting a meeting in June. 'We also met sympathetic MPs who advised setting a tone of cooperation not hostility. We didn't want to attack MPs and stand outside parliament shouting. Instead we gave them plenty of advance warning of the lobby so they could appreciate the issues and have a proper discussion.' The TJM coordinated the work of coalition groups making sure, for instance, that each sent out publicity materials and that speakers were booked for the rallies.

The budget was just £65,000 – compared to £1 million for the Countryside Alliance march. TJM's letter-writing campaign raised so much interest that the prime minister, Tony Blair, who had rejected a call for a meeting, changed his mind and met representatives on the morning of the lobby. The trade and industry minister, Patricia Hewitt, and the select committee on international development also asked the TJM to address them.

On the day, 12,000 people formed a queue stretching from parliament, over the Thames and along the South Bank. MPs agreed to come outside because many people would not have been able to get past Commons security checks to see them. Holt continues: 'An hour into the lobby I walked along the line and every few yards there was a big cluster of people with their MP in the centre answering questions.' The TJM also experimented with text messaging, largely to raise morale as people waited for their MP. Lobbyists had to sign up to the scheme in advance, agreeing to be 'spammed' by the TJM on the day. It proved a hit when organisers were able to pass on a message of support from the South African president, Thabo Mbeki. It also gave the running total of MPs lobbied, which reached 346 – more than half of the entire parliament.

In reality of course the best campaigns use a mixture of placed features, news reportage, paid advertising and direct response marketing devices. The mix is crucial and should not be rigidly budget-driven though it is accepted that in many not-for-profits budgets are inevitably very tight. Remarkable buys however are often available for tactical advertising if contingency plans have been made.

# Ethical questions

Working with a corporate is of course one way of expanding available budgets, providing that the collaboration is appropriate and doesn't raise ethical questions. For example most development charities will not work with Nestlé because of their continued inappropriate promotion of dried babyfood products. However Shelter, operating with homeless people in the UK, has deemed some sponsorship from Nestlé acceptable. But what happens when a commercial company seeks the moral high ground? Are charities facing competition from ethical businesses?

'One toy a child will pick up once and never play with again.' This national newspaper advertisement, apparently campaigning against the user of cluster bombs, looks like a traditional not-for-profit advertisement. The stark picture, clever headline, and powerful text are clearly influenced by years of successful newspaper appeals by the likes of Amnesty International and other campaigning groups.

Yet this advertisement has been placed by Co-operative Bank which is campaigning to call for a freeze on the use of cluster bombs. The advertisement encourages readers to sign the Bank's online petition, or 'make a donation that will go straight towards clearance programmes to help communities return to a normal way of life'. You have to read the small print at the bottom to find that 'for details of how your money will be spent please ask in branch or see our website'.

The Co-operative Bank is working in conjunction with Landmine Action, the 50-strong coalition of voluntary organisations involved with the issue of landmines. It is supporting the campaign as part of its ethical policy and the advertisements appeared as part of Landmine Action Week in 2002.

This is not a one-off development. Speaking at a Blackbaud European Conference for Not-for-profits in London, consultant Daryl Upsall warned that commercial organisations could start to take on some of the roles of charities. He suggested that 'it will become harder for the public to distinguish ethical business from charity'.

## ... And what about sex?

Commercial advertisers have for many years used sex to help sell products and services, and to differentiate brands. The car industry has used scantily clad models to help launch new cars for decades and advertisements featuring alluring actors have been a mainstay of many a manufacturer's promotional programme. Although this approach is now deemed unacceptable to women, as demeaning and reinforcing sexual stereotypes, it still goes on albeit with rather more subtle themes and executions.

A Kodak advertisement in the autumn of 2002 showed a handsome young man leaving a photo of himself on the pillow of his attractive female partner with the message, 'I'd rather be here'. Mobile phone advertisements tout the pleasure of flirting via text messages. Renault Clio advertisements show father and daughter both keeping assignations, and driving sporty little cars. Sex continues to be used by advertisers to put over images of attractive lifestyles, building brand recognition and helping to sell product. So where in all this are the not-for-profits?

It might be thought that that the two are mutually exclusive. But are they? The answer has to be a resounding 'yes ... and no'. Passion is a deep vital element in life and love, its power is there to be harnessed in the service of good causes. Bob Geldof's passionate plea, 'just give us the fucking money' at the Live Aid concert in 1985 is unforgettable. It is aggressive, powerful and seductive. The Band Aid record that preceded the concert happened because Geldof himself had been watching television scenes of the terrible famine in Ethiopia. He was moved to tears, vowed to do something and the best selling single 'Do they know it's Christmas?' was the direct result. Geldof's passion persuaded dozens of prominent musicians and celebrities to perform, or record messages of support.

However it is debatable whether sexual passion has a place in most not-for-profit's marketing strategy. As advertisers have learned, the brand needs to be seen overtly or by association as being desirable, alluring and sexy. This can work for chocolate and cars but seems improbable for good causes. Nevertheless as Mark Astarita points out (see Chapter nine), without passion it becomes hard to differentiate one children's charity from another or an animal sanctuary from a wildlife conservation trust. Aggression, anger, outrage, desperation are all powerful, appropriate emotions for those seeking to communicate the messages of the not-for-profit. Those can and should evoke passion in the communicator and the recipient. That passion is a vital part of a successful organisation's differentiation and the unique nature of a cause. The call to action must then becomes irresistible. The call to action through sexual attraction, though extremely potent can, usually, be resisted.

# Which audience, which message?

Within the planning process decisions need to be made about the split between advertising and editorial. In the same way issues of 'which audience segment need to receive which part of the message(s)' must be thought through well in advance of the campaign implementation plan since this will dictate timings and media selection. For example long-term supporters of a charity and even potential supporters with the same age profile and demographic background may well have an existing high awareness of the organisation, the cause and the needs involved. The messages within an advertisement placed in *Saga* may be quite different to those destined for the *Big Issue*. The messages within reports or press releases aimed at either will also need to have quite different emphases to appeal to the very different audience. One size clearly does not fit all. Segmentation has to be at the heart of these considerations, followed by analysis and agreement to the desired outcomes.

Even where the principal message remains the same, for coherence and impact, then it is likely that different executions of both adverts and media releases should be considered to gain the maximum exposure and impact. For example the 'Symptoms' campaign created by the advertising agency Kilmartin-Baker for the then British Diabetic Association was enormously successful in both raising awareness of the early symptoms of diabetes, and (if experiencing them) the need to visit a doctor as well as helping to double membership over four years. One of the keys to success was the use of differing advertisement executions depending upon the media carrying it: Figure 16 shows the generic advertisement, whilst Figure 17 shows an example aimed at London commuters.

**FIGURE 16** EXAMPLE OF BDA'S GENERIC ADVERTISING

Always going to the loo, always thirsty, always tired?

You could be suffering from a form of diabetes.
Ask your own doctor for a test – diagnosis and simple treatment could quickly restore your old sparkle.

**BRITISH DIABETIC ASSOCIATION**
10 QUEEN ANNE STREET, LONDON W1M 0BD. REG. CHARITY No. 215199.

For more information
**FREEPHONE 0800 60 70 60.**

Fighting to free Britain from Diabetes.

**FIGURE 17** EXAMPLE OF BDA'S SEGMENTED ADVERTISING

# Is always feeling tired and thirsty, always going to the loo, stopping you from being a City highflyer?

You could be suffering from a form of diabetes. Ask your doctor for a test –
diagnosis and simple treatment could quickly restore your old sparkle.

## BRITISH DIABETIC ASSOCIATION
10 QUEEN ANNE STREET, LONDON W1M 0BD. REG. CHARITY No. 215199.
A charity helping people with diabetes and supporting diabetes research

For more information
**FREEPHONE 0800 60 70 60.**

## The power of the message

Charities generally have a huge advantage when it comes to developing and communicating brand values. When it comes to changing

the world not-for-profits can grab the attention. The range is enormous, from Battersea Dogs Home saving and rehoming stray animals to Friends of the Earth who are out to save the planet. The ideas and values conveyed must be readily identifiable and in harmony with the mission so that programmes can developed to communicate them effectively with the organisation's chosen audiences.

The Cystic Fibrosis Trust, for example, has launched an appeal for £15 million which, if successful, could see the charity almost cease to exist in five years time; scientists estimate that with the appropriate investment a cure for cystic fibrosis may be only five years away. Of course most medical research charities have claimed for decades that a cure may be, 'just around the corner'. However if the appeal is communicated effectively a new case for support will be created and makes for a very powerful, positive message.

# Use of the Internet

The last ten years has seen a revolution in the way that organisations, but especially not-for-profits, use the Internet and construct websites to assist their communications objectives. First generation sites were usually no more than digital brochures, describing the organisation and its work. Response, if invited, was generally via phone or traditional letter. Second generation sites attempted some interactivity and implemented E-mail links to improve response handling. They also began to integrate site management into marketing and communications strategies. Most organisations are now learning that their presence on the Internet is not simply an important part of an effective marketing strategy; crucially, they are beginning to understand that they must consider the audiences viewing it even more carefully than when they create a brochure, mail shot or other publication. Integration of the look, feel and messages broadcast by the site is crucial to avoid inconsistencies and contradictions.

For some time Oxfam has been one of the leading not-for-profit exponents of Internet use. As Andrew Hatton comments: 'Our website has moved from being about Oxfam GB to being Oxfam GB.' This is a important distinction. First time visitors get an immediate feel that is replicated in their literature and advertising. Navigation is not only simple but immediately informative and invitations to join E-mail listings are hard to resist. Permission is actively sought for text messaging to mobile phones and clearly the communication plan to back up such proactive data collection has been carefully developed and implemented.

Howard Lake, director of Fundraising UK, the leading Internet information resource for fundraisers comments: 'There are still very few charities using E-mail effectively, to communicate.' He goes on: 'There is an urgent need to build confidence and competence. People must build in-house expertise by getting their hands dirty because Internet product lifecycles are getting shorter and the only way to keep abreast is to try it!' His view is that campaigning organisations are learning how to create and use micro-sites to improve campaign reach and effectiveness but that this is generally restricted to the larger not-for-profits.

# Internal audiences

Internal understanding and ownership is as important to reaching an audience, if not more so, than the implementation of an external communications plan. Where stakeholders buy in to advertising plans and projects, they start with a much better chance of success. Without prior knowledge and understanding how can staff react to comment and act as brand champions? For not-for-profit organisations the mobilisation of their volunteer network with a united and coherent understanding of the desired communication objectives can be the factor that differentiates success from failure.

Jeremy Prescott, managing director of Citigate Albert Frank, puts it succinctly: 'If internally the objectives are not clearly communicated and understood what earthly chance is there of anyone else understanding the message?' He is quite candid about the role of an agency in helping charities in particular understand their markets saying: 'It's up to an agency to do a market audit, without charging the client, in order to really understand the brand.' Internal audiences must be considered at an early stage and engaged in challenging ways to ensure consistency.

Overall then, each internal audience – board, management, staff, volunteers and others – need to be as carefully considered as the external ones. These in turn include: existing and potential customers, service users, clients, suppliers, supporters, investors, regulators, policy makers and legislative influencers and indeed any other group or segment that the organisation is interested in communicating with.

# Conclusion

In considering the marketeer's audiences and how to reach them it is vital to analyse carefully the desired outcomes, ensure they are realistic and achievable and then go about constructing strategies that will deliver the goods.

It is only after successfully conveying a message internally that messages can reach chosen external audiences effectively, and with any realistic chance of achieving corporate objectives. As discussed in Chapter three (see p52), both for-profit and not-for-profit organisations have to consider internal audiences as a vital segment of their target audiences.

# CHAPTER NINE

# The future of marketing

'The best way to predict the future is to invent it.'   *Dr Alan Kay*

'Be the change you want to see in the world.'   *Mahatma Gandhi*

How will for-profits and not-for-profits be operating by 2020? And, even more important, how will not-for-profits rise to meet the marketing challenges of the next decade? This chapter draws on the visions of several leading figures and commentators in the voluntary sector to answer some of these questions, and offer a provocative picture of the years to come.

## Perspectives

The government's strategy unit finally published their long-awaited report in September 2002 and closed the book on comments in December of that year. Whilst the report is a consultative document, indications of the shape of things to come are now clearer. Questions remain, however: how much of the report will be acted upon and how many of the 61 recommendations will have the necessary legislation or regulatory powers enabled, in order for them to become a reality? Charities are, for example, desperate for clarification of issues relating to street collections in order to address concerns over reduced public confidence.

Much of what actually emerges in the form of imposed regulation, as opposed to self-regulation, depends upon the will of the government during the remainder of their second term in office. As the following two sections demonstrate, both government and opposition are in accord over a number of the issues but questions remain over the will of the present or future government to make progress on many others. The year 2010 seems close in terms of planning timeframes but in political terms it will fall either at the end of the current government's third term, or at the end of a new government's first term.

# The government's view

The current government has much to say on forthcoming changes as a result of the reviews it has conducted. The charities minister, Lord Filkin, has already made it his personal mission to make sure that nothing – especially local government – impedes the implementation of the reviews. In particular he is taking a personal lead in addressing local authorities about the conclusions of the cross-cutting review. This looked at impediments to voluntary and community organisations delivering public services – pointing out that between 1997 and 2002 there was a significant expansion of the private sector in the delivery of publicly-funded services.

He has also promised to address personally the issue of local government contracts, adding that: 'Intelligent procurement and intelligent partnership with the voluntary sector is what we have got to discuss with local government and central government departments.'

He believes that the combination of being local, flexible and trustworthy may give not-for-profit organisations a 'competitive advantage in terms of getting better outcomes for the public'. These services could fit neatly into one of the suggestions of the strategy unit's review of charity regulation, which is to set up a new legal form of community interest companies (CICs). However he does not expect CICs to become monolithic and start running significant numbers of local services. 'Instead of the old model of essentially a large ship delivering public service – a government department or local authority – we are much more interested in a range of suppliers.'

Lord Filkin regards the strategy unit's review of charity regulation as a report to government, not necessarily the government's stated policy. For example he does not believe that public schools will lose charitable status. Furthermore he believes that the issue of relieving charities of irrecoverable VAT is dead stating that, 'we couldn't see that there was a practical or adequate reason to exempt charities'.

Regarding proposed changes to the Charity Commission's role, he believes that it is important for the Commission to move with the times and be seen to be fit for its purpose. 'In terms of open AGMs, there is a style issue of a public body being open to discussion and debate. It is important to increase the openness and accessibility of a crucial public body like the Charity Commission.' To this end, he also agrees with the idea of an independent tribunal, feeling that it would be a lot cheaper than appealing to the high court against Charity Commission decisions. With regard to recommendations on standardised annual returns of statistical information and the performance of charities, the review team and Lord Filkin are both adamant this will not lead to league tables in the same way that schools, hospitals and local councils are being subjected to star ratings.

The stance is firm: 'I wouldn't expect to see league tables because the government doesn't have a set of objectives in the same way as it does say for secondary schools. There is no agenda for the charity and voluntary sector. Apart from thinking in principle that the government has got a duty to create an environment in which individuals will volunteer, get together at a local or national level to work towards the improvement of civic society or to campaign for change.' It seems likely therefore that although the Treasury review is trying to bring voluntary and community organisations into the same overall fold, in terms of public service delivery, charities will be able to hold on to the privileged status of remaining independent and free from star ratings. However, some might, and do, say that this would allow charities to avoid playing by the same rules.

Similarly in the face of public outrage and press criticism about the inappropriate way in which corporates have acted, Margaret Beckett, secretary of state for the environment, food and rural affairs, has hardened the government's stance on corporate ethics. Adding to existing promises of further regulation to prevent companies acting outside the public good, this is an additional wake-up call to all for-profit organisations to get their houses in order and take corporate social responsibility far more seriously.

# The opposition's view

The Conservative party leader, Iain Duncan Smith, has spelt out an curiously similar approach to that of the government and within days of publication of the strategy unit's report called on the government to introduce a charities bill to push forward charity reform. He announced that the Conservatives would also be seeking a greater role for the voluntary sector in the delivery of public services. He says the party would, 'identify ways in which the voluntary sector can be given access to a wider range of projects currently funded and executed by arms of government'. He added that, 'the understanding gained will shape our plans for reform of the public services and lead to more diverse provision'. He has said that his party would review funding mechanisms.

Mr Duncan Smith has also lent his support to the NCVO call for a charities bill to package together changes to charity law. Stephen Bubb, the chief executive of Association for Chief Executives of Voluntary Organisations (ACEVO) has commented that: 'It is excellent to get cross-party support for charity reform and we welcome Iain Duncan Smith's support for a charity bill as otherwise the proposed reforms could easily slip off the agenda.' He added that the Conservatives were going further than Labour in wanting the voluntary sector to run schools and hospitals; however he warned that charities should not be seen as a cheap option. 'If charities are funded correctly that is fine but we don't want to be a football with the unions arguing that we are taking jobs from the public sector.'

Overall then it appears that many of the recommendations will be enforced either through regulation or additional primary legislation. This will see not-for-profits playing a larger role in the delivery of a wider range of services than is currently the case, an indication perhaps that many already sizeable charities will become substantially larger and less dependent upon voluntary income. Conversely this may lead to further public resistance to supporting such organisations which could be seen increasingly as organs of government, unless attempts to build public trust and confidence, through greater transparency, clarity and openness, are successful. Once again those organisations able to capitalise most effectively upon their brands (their reputations) are likely to be the winners whilst the medium-sized charities and those not able or willing to market themselves effectively will be the losers.

## 'High tech, high touch'

Tony Cram, MBA programme director at Ashridge Management College, has some intriguing suggestions: 'Ethics are for real!' His view is that whilst many corporates have been investing in social auditing and improved environmental impact assessments, the next few years will see a much greater emphasis on operating, and being seen to operate, ethically. This he goes on, 'will be a real challenge and opportunity for charities to work alongside companies helping develop and implement some of those programmes'. Cram also suggests that changes in the regulator regime may be more wide-reaching than many commentators predict. He feels for example that trustees will have the same pressures upon them as non-executive directors have today.

With the continuing growth in technology and technical solutions to problems, marketing or otherwise, Cram suggests that the challenge for all organisations will be to embrace a culture of 'high tech, and high touch'. By this he means that whilst more technology is used to run systems and administer marketing programmes, the winners will be those who are able to keep close to customers and clients. This is the 'high touch' or, as Ken Burnett (2002) suggests in the title of his book *Relationship Fundraising*, ensuring that audiences can get as close to the organisation they are dealing with as they want. 'Those who rely on technology alone will be the losers,' Burnett suggests, particularly as it will become much harder to manage images and reputations because there will be far more 'touch points'. Every time a customer or supporter has any sort of contact, through advertising, editorial, passive observation, active conversation, Internet, telephone, cinema, video and DVD, with an organisation by seeing, hearing, or conversing about its brand, this is a touch point and an opportunity to impress, bore or actively discourage. Organisations, especially not-for-profits, will have to think through their approach to integrating communications much more rigorously to avoid dissonance between all these touch points.

Cram has a final challenge for corporates and charities to work more profitably together. 'With the increasing global view of markets it's not just international charities who will need to form international alliances. There will be opportunities for effectively local or UK only not-for-profits to work with European and even world-wide partners, to deliver real local benefits in the markets that a global company is seeking to operate and grow.' He adds however, 'charities will have to seek out talent and communicate much more effectively. Where there's scarcity salaries grow disproportionately – perhaps alternative creative solutions will come from the voluntary sector, since collaborations based on addressing issues of mutual self-interest are always likely to be more effective.'

# The shape of things to come

Simon Burne is chair of the Institute of Fundraising and director of fundraising at the children's charity NCH. He is of the opinion that: 'Forecasting ten years into the future is likely to be about as useful as unravelling the pronouncements of the oracle at Delphi or peering at sheep's entrails was to the ancient Greeks.' He adds: 'But it's also pretty safe: I'd be surprised if anyone comes back to me in ten years and tells me I got it all wrong!' There are however some very clear trends.

The public is moving from supporting charities to supporting causes. This has enormous implications for charities. There will be increasing pressure on charities to form coalitions or to merge so that charity equals cause. Current strategy unit proposals will make this easier. Cause marketing will take over from charity marketing. We will see virtual charities – those existing only in name to channel resources to their member organisations.

Causes and issues will rise and fall in the public consciousness increasingly fast, as the media become ever more central to forming public opinion. Cause marketing, therefore, will have to become very much more fleet of foot to capture the hearts and minds of existing and potential supporters.

Linked to this public fickleness will be the increasing ease and confidence with which the public can start and stop payments to charities. Customer care may well not be enough in the future, and charities will have to explore new ways to develop loyalty marketing. At the same time, there's no doubt that regulation will increase over this period. Charity marketing methods will become more subject to scrutiny and monitoring, which may restrict innovation and will almost certainly push up costs.

The number of marketing channels for both awareness raising and fundraising will continue to explode with individual channels rising and falling more rapidly than ever. There will be a great increase in community channels on radio and digital TV. With this rise, there will be a segmentation of markets to the extent that mass audiences will become a thing of the past. This has advantages in as far as charities can identify their segments clearly. But there's no doubt that the communications mix will become a complicated cocktail.

Traditional supporters will fade away – successful marketeers will develop ways to reach out to and retain new supporters. Direct dialogue fundraising has led the way here and will continue to do so, but more marketing will take place over the mobile telephone and, of course, on the Internet. New fundraising products need to be offered to these new supporters; something to replace international challenge events which will decline.

The winners in all this will be those local charities possessing a strong local presence and national and international charities possessing a clearly defined cause-related brand and recognition. The losers will be smaller national or international charities that fail to merge or join coalitions and causes that do not match the public agenda.

## What won't change

A decade on, the objective of communicating effectively with an organisation's chosen audiences will remain, and so people will continue to occupy most marketeers' attention. Customer relationship marketing (CRM) systems may become a great deal more refined and, as Tony Cram postulates, charities and corporates will probably spend far more of their time and energy preserving relationships with their top 20 per cent of customers and supporters. Some of the techniques may change to allow greater analysis and the refinement of customer profiling, but the basic practices remain as effective today as they were in 1990 or will be in 2010. People give to people. Customers buy and, given half a chance, will continue to buy from sales staff.

The analogue TV system may have been turned off by 2010 but many consumers will simply have invested in set-top decoders. The integration of PC and television has a way to go yet. And even when it has come about there will still be people watching and making decisions to purchase or not.

## A provocative picture

The pace of real change, even taking technology into account, is often far slower than we think (or hope) it will be. How much did UK society change in the ten years between 1990 and 2000? How much did the regulatory framework change? It's true that the government changed from the Thatcher years of 1979 to 1990 to a New Labour government in 1997 but many have observed that New Labour pledged to continue Conservative economic policy over the first three years. Many also believe that they have continued this policy into their second term. A third term would see them into 2006 so would 2010 see them, tired and devoid of inspiration, at the end of a third term? Or perhaps some other party will be stumbling into an election run up after a precarious first term? The political environment will be one of the key predictors of the rate of change for not-for-profits and for-profits alike. However for not-for-profits that work closely with government, and depend upon fees, grants and central funding for many of their activities, the framework within which they work and the policies of the government directing investment and expenditure will be crucial.

The current Labour government, in their second term, have talked expansively of a greater role for the voluntary sector, providing more services and receiving more of their infrastructure costs in return. If this actually happens we could see a rapid growth of the existing major players such as Barnardo's, NCH and NSPCC in the field of childcare, RNIB, RNID, Scope and Mencap working with disabled people, and Help the Aged and British Legion, together with some commercial providers, working with the elderly. Mergers with many small- to medium-sized providers are likely as the true costs of meeting the 2002 Care Standards Act become reality and seriously under-funded private and charity providers seek solutions to their needs for long-term investment. Many providers, commercial and charity, are making strident representations about the enormous costs involved in meeting the new standards and the need to be flexible over existing facilities. Hence the government may well back-track on some mandatory requirements, particularly for existing provision. Indeed, it has already softened its stance over certain standards being advisory rather than compulsory. The die is cast, however, and expectations of great improvements will not go away. In a not dissimilar way, as noted in Chapter one, universities and other higher education institutes are also looking for mergers in order to compete more successfully for funding.

## A view from the boundary

Kate Nash is the chief executive of RADAR and a passionate advocate for the empowerment of disabled people. Her views concerning the disability movement are probably just as applicable to any other minority grouping. Each form very important customer and supporter audiences as well as being potential beneficiaries of the services of many not-for-profits. The structure of RADAR itself may be a portent of the way in which more charities will come to work together. It is part of a new group structure, with the 'Enabling Partnership' at the hub, as a unique driver for change in the voluntary sector that enables disability charities to be more effective. The Enabling Partnership undertakes activities that are common to all organisations, making it possible for individual charities to be more effective in their core missions.

Fundraising, marketing and communications, human resources, finance and IT are all costly functions that are at the heart of any effective organisation. The group provides these pivotal, shared resources, so releasing funds and avoiding duplication. Member organisations can focus on their charitable objectives, and therefore better serve the aspirations of disabled people. Current members of the Enabling Partnership are The Enham Trust, The Royal Association for Disability and Rehabilitation (RADAR), the National Federation of Shopmobility UK (NFSUK) and Holiday Care. The National Information Forum has also voted to join and discussions are being held with several other not-for-profits.

Nash believes that it is likely that disability charities will appear and operate very differently in the year 2010. This is partly because of the need to function more efficiently as above, and partly about the need to respond differently and appropriately to the emergence of disability as a rights issue, rather than a charitable one. Twenty years after the introduction of race and gender legislation, disability legislation is starting to permeate the social consciousness of the business and statutory sector. The notion of reasonable adjustments will have, by then, become common parlance and as such, new ways will need to be found to 'sell' disability as a charitable cause.

By 2010 there may well be fresh energy from the disability movement and in particular the Disability Rights Commission to put pressure on the Charity Commission to 'relinquish' its hold on disability. Relinquishing its hold might force new models of thought and create change in the natural public response to disability. By encouraging society away from being instinctively philanthropic towards seeing disability as a rights issue, the Charity Commission might well be able to enhance disabled people's prospects of social inclusion.

Added to that is the fact that there is a 'coming together' of human difference. The government is looking to merge the Equal Opportunities Commission, Disability Rights Commission and Commission for Racial Equality. And while, if this happens, it is unlikely that any merger will take effect until 2008, disability charities will by then be responding to new ideas about how the world accepts human difference. It is not for nothing that RADAR's vision is of a society in which human difference is routinely anticipated, expertly accommodated and positively celebrated.

Marketeers will need to consider complex social constructs and indeed have always needed to do so: Nash points out that in the case of disability marketeers have not always done so, but that most disability charities worth their salt have now moved well away from sad images of disabled people who are in desperate need of the public's spare cash.

Equally, in 2010 marketing messages will need to be constructed for a distinctly different climate. The Disability Discrimination Act (DDA) 1995 was designed to try to end discrimination against disabled people. While its remit is limited, and the powers of the DRC likewise, what it may well have done by 2010 is change the context within which disabled people are campaigning. As a result, the way in which disability organisations campaign and deliver services must change too. Gaining reasonable adjustments in the workplace is one thing. Tackling profound and deep-routed assumptions about the value of life of disabled people is quite another.

Once upon a time, in a different but far from dissimilar context, gay rights campaigner Tom Robinson sang: 'the buggers are legal now, what more are they after?' Marketeers, on behalf of disability organisations, will need to know the answer as well as find enticing ways of convincing a range of audiences that the need for change remains, the appetite for further work is acute and the achievability is real. The coming together of disability organisations with other similar interest groups may well be one very effective response to this challenge.

# A call to action

Mark Astarita of NDCS has a rather different view of how things might develop for marketeers. He believes that the public face of most charities is, more often that not, carried through its fundraising messages. Some will argue that this is as a direct consequence of the need to focus the potential donor audience on a call to action. Usually this call will be in the form of giving money, and so there is a narrowing of the charity's brand down to a simple request for support. As a result of the techniques employed by fundraisers being broadly similar in most charities (and for that matter donor types more often than not being similar in terms of characteristics and demographics), the methods of communication end up looking similar. Key messages will not overly differ whether money is raised for animals, youth, disability or overseas development.

So why shouldn't the principal vehicle by which people understand the brand values of a charity be narrowed down to its sales proposition? Is it altogether a bad thing and is it likely to change much? It seems probable that fundraising expenditure is unlikely to diminish as a total proportion of charitable expenditure and may in fact increase in a competitive environment. Examine the annual report of any major charity and fundraising expenditure will almost always take second place ahead of everything except the primary purpose, charitable spend.

# The importance of cause

Not-for-profits are one of the largest users of direct mail in the UK. Fundraisers are now beginning to turn their attention, some with great success, to direct response television. Many argue that charity brands need to operate more like the commercial sector. Why do you buy your Cola from Coca-Cola rather than from Virgin? Why not simply buy the supermarket own brand at a lower price?

However, charities are *not* selling the same product; they are simply using the same techniques by which to make that sale. The NDCS, for example, provides a variety of services for the nation's 35,000 deaf children and is very different in approach to the RNID or NSPCC, yet all three may well deploy the very same techniques in acquiring new donors or support. It seems unlikely that people buy brands in relation to charities. It is more certain that they buy causes and the way in which vision and mission are described for the cause will be the vital key to unlocking that support.

# Addressing individuals

It is not surprising that someone who has had a relation die from cancer or a heart attack will choose related causes when they consider which charities to support with a legacy; health charities do particularly well from legacy income. Personal circumstances matter here more than hard-hitting campaigns. Longevity and history are also factors; many of today's biggest charities have been around for a long time and that the older generation who grew up with these charities should give to them is also not surprising.

Yet until recently Oxfam, one of the best known charities, received only £8 million in legacies whilst Barnardo's, by comparison, received £21 million. Will that trend continue in the future as the 'baby boomer' generation begin to leave their legacies to charity? There may be a seismic change in charitable donations; they might not reduce in value or volume, but they may well go to very different causes than currently. For some charities the doomsday scenario lies in the baby boomers, who may have very different brand preferences and attitudes to their own.

Does anyone believe that people will not begin to leave money to Comic Relief and Children in Need? Will our development charities, which have often proved to be the most successful and pioneering fundraisers charities from the living, not begin to reap the rewards of legacies, so that Oxfam, Save the Children and others take the lion's share of such income in the future? The charities that will be successful in legacy fundraising will be those that are asking, not those that are waiting for people to give. Dorothy Donor is dying out and attention must turn to the Daniels, Jasons, Emmas and Sarahs who will be the future donors. Yet for too long supporter databases have failed to allow people to be addressed as individuals. Everyone has purchased broadly similar lists of people to whom to address direct mail.

Technique will drive the method by which people give in the future. Direct mail works for an older generation who like the emotional ask more often than not contained within traditional charity direct mail. However in an increasingly secular world where people's belief in organised religion wanes dramatically, could charities adopt an ask appealing to social 'feel-good' factors to replace such belief? It is possible that in the not too distant future a majority may no longer believe in an after-life and instead seek satisfaction in making a difference to this one. Such changes in social priorities now take place over relatively short periods; after all, to the UK population only 30 years ago a holiday abroad was an expensive luxury, the exception rather than the rule. Now it is generally regarded as part of normal family expenditure.

The human race has not changed greatly. Human civilisation was born out of the necessity to cooperate. It has been in our interests as human beings not to 'walk on by'. Many believe altruism is a basic survival instinct. Not-for-profits today have a marvellous opportunity to fill a gap, a particular need in everyone's psyche, to do something worthwhile, to make a real difference, to help change lives for the better.

This need is only ever triggered to any meaningful extent when a charity places before an individual both the opportunity to make a difference and the method by which they can do that, more often than not by making a donation as their pact with hope and a future. So while direct mail will work with some and DRTV with others, face-to-face and direct dialogue fundraising will be put to work with a different generation.

## Harnessing inspiration

The corporate sector is increasingly trying to gain ground by borrowing the social agenda; witness Shell advertisements on protecting the environment, or others in the field of technology that show developing countries making use of technology to communicate. The message is clear: the corporate sector is beginning to learn that a social agenda and the ability to motivate and inspire consumers to think differently is a sure fire way to enhance brand reputations.

Not-for-profits have nothing to be shy of in this arena. 'Never be afraid to ask': you could give an individual, who has been asked to support, a wonderful feeling. The art of great fundraising is to use the technique that first elicits attention, then produces some kind of action and finally, slowly but surely, inspires that individual or organisation to believe as strongly as the charity in its ultimate mission. For charities to change hearts and minds they must forever be stretching the boundaries of credibility and possibility. They must treat everyone as an individual and tailor requests and offers to that individual's keenest desires, while never losing sight of the fact that the driving force behind a charity's mission is the needs and interests of its beneficiaries, not its donors.

Astarita comments that currently the hallmark of most donors' actions is that of 'giving and forgetting'. They give when they're asked and they don't necessarily want a long and beautiful relationship with any one charity. Many donors enjoy the fact that a number of small donations makes them feel a lot better, believing that they are making a difference to many and varied causes. Astarita therefore feels that marketeers must concentrate firepower, effort and attention on those most likely to give for *whatever* reason. In this case too, inspiration and determination to share the passion are key. The brand values of a charity are only as valuable as the effort put in by everyone concerned, from frontline staff to fundraisers and trustees, from the volunteer in the shop to the receptionist on the front counter. They must all smile a welcoming smile and show a passionate belief in what they're doing. Those charities displaying this behaviour will be the leaders in 2010 and their beneficiaries the winners.

Tony Manwaring, the former director of fundraising at NCH and now chief executive at Scope, says: 'Charities are at their best when they create a bridge between past, present and future; giving life to the values of those who were moved to set them up, providing a vehicle by which their mission can be achieved in today's society, whilst offering a message of hope and a model for transformation. In this, fundraising and marketing are inextricably linked.' He goes on to conclude that: 'Fundraising is more than about money. It is also the currency of people's desire to make a difference, to make the world a better place. And marketing – at its best – provides the toolkit for a common language which gives that hope form, moving hearts as well as minds. Together, they provide the lever that can enable charities to give people a glimpse of a better future – and thereby to create tomorrow, today.'

# Encouraging the legacy

The Legacy campaign 'Remember a Charity' is the work of a consortium of nearly 100 charities launched with the objective of increasing the percentage of those remembering a favourite charity in their wills. Smee and Ford's figures (Legacy Foresight 2002) indicate that up to 2001 some 13.2 per cent of wills proved in England and Wales contained charitable bequests and that the average will mentioned something like 2.8 organisations. Whilst the number of charitable bequests has risen over 20 years from around two per will to nearly three, no amount of individual charity legacy promotion had had any significant effect on the numbers of people making any mention of charities in their wills. The campaign grew out of a challenge by George Smith (then chairman of advertising agency Smith Bundy) in 1994 to the fundraising directors of 20 or so larger charities. He said: 'If around a third of the UK population give regularly to charity and less than half of them mention you in their wills then you've got a problem with the legacy as a fundraising product!' He went on to add that as an advertising man he would advocate a major campaign initiative to challenge people's perceptions of legacy bequests, educate those making wills and persuade more of them to write in favourite causes. He challenged those senior managers to find the ways and means to address what all agreed was a crucial funding question for the sector.

The group worked on the challenge for some considerable time, trying to conduct research and gain widespread agreement to some form of coordinated campaign. The result was the Legacy campaign, the public face of which, 'Remember a Charity', was launched in September 2002 (see Figure 13, p106). Research conducted on behalf of the consortium revealed the 13 per cent of those who make wills that go to probate who write in a charitable bequest. If the campaign is successful in increasing the percentage to 15 then by the end of the decade another £3 billion per annum might be available to charities for their core and development needs.

This in turn may lead to many more established charities (the best known and trusted are the ones most likely to benefit from generic campaigns) branching out into new areas, perhaps in partnership with local and central government to cover areas currently provided by the state. Distribution of any significant increases will not be even and could, perhaps, lead to more aggressive takeovers rather than mergers of other charities struggling with financial survival, though the Charity Commission would need to adopt a far more proactive role in allowing such amalgamations to occur.

# Planned change

## Planned giving

One of the changes that will happen in the UK is the migration from the USA of 'planned giving'. In the USA it is reported (Sargeant and Lee 2003) that up to 40 per cent of voluntary income derives from planned giving initiatives. The huge difference between this and legacy gifts is that a planned gift is legally provided for in the life-time of the donor and that whilst the recipient not-for-profit organ-isation has an interest in the gift it does not gain the full benefit until a deferred point – often the death of the donor. Financial prod-ucts suitable for the UK market need to be designed and financial services organisations will need to work very closely with charities to promote the benefits to prospective donors whose knowledge and understanding of the tax implications lags way behind that of USA counterparts.

Nevertheless with the Giving campaign taking a lead on such issues, and with government support for the necessary regulatory regimes, it seems as if planned giving is one of the few certainties that will see substantial growth and mutual benefit for participating com-panies and charities alike over the next decade. The USA model will almost certainly not be replicated but a version suitable for differ-ent behaviour, culture and beliefs will make quite an impression.

## In memoriam giving

Even more exciting may be developments in the use of memorial or tribute funds aimed at involving supporters who make 'in memor-iam' donations.

'In memoriam' giving, whereby people make donations in memory of friends and loved ones, is currently much neglected. Charities have generally had few ideas about how to cultivate such support. In February 2003, however, not-for-profit marketing agency White-water attempted to change all that. Their ideas may put 'in memor-iam' fundraising centre stage; the agency has developed strategies which may change the way in which people give to charity forever.

Charities will set up Tribute Funds named after the people who have passed away. Donors will have a vehicle through which to donate and raise money, forever, in the name of the person they have lost. This strategy aims to bring charity giving closer to people's hearts, to inspire people to give more and raise more. And it could bring to the world of charity giving people who have not responded to other appeals to date. What is more, it could bring a new generation of younger supporters to various causes; they tend to ignore direct mail, but will they ignore the fund named after 'grandad'?

Whitewater believe that these totally unrestricted funds will generate long-term income streams and ultimately significantly increase legacy income. Managing director Steve Andrews says, 'the possibilities are endless ... This is an approach with the capacity to increase the numbers of in memoriam donors and then dramatically increase their lifetime values. It's giving donors what they want!'

The next decade will see real movement in this area and potentially change the face of relationship fundraising for ever. Even where charities do not adopt proactive strategies to promotes these named funds a revised, more appropriate, approach to 'in memoriam' donations (which according to Whitewater's research already yields £30 million per annum) should increase the numbers and values very significantly.

## Mixed joint campaigns

As discussed in Chapters seven and eight, charities generally have distinct advantages when it comes to developing and delivering communications strategies. Strong, urgent, powerful messages can be constructed and delivered whatever medium is chosen. Increasingly multimedia will be the norm. Here again there is a huge opportunity for commercial marketeers to use some of their far more substantial promotional budgets creatively, providing innovative solutions and propositions for customers and supporters alike. An excellent recent example is that of the Triodos Bank piggy-backing on the well recognised ethical reputations of Amnesty International and Oxfam to reinforce their own ethical philosophy and practices. Much greater use of mixed joint campaigns will surely follow.

The ability of not-for-profits to reach fragmented but highly motivated audiences will be crucial in all this. Their understanding and use of the changing channels of communication will be a major factor in determining who succeeds and who is left behind.

## Conclusion

In reality of course only time will tell what the marketing challenges will be. Most certainly the world may change a lot less than we think. Conversely Tim Berners-Lee (a former president of the RSA and one of the worldwide web pioneers) is quoted as saying on the

'Random quotes' website: 'If we know what the future is we aren't looking far enough ahead.' A few years ago a number of contributors to a Third Sector publication (*From Mailshots to the Millennium* 1995) tried to look ahead and make predictions about what might be happening in five to ten years time: John Rodd for example postulated that in 2000 Abel Newman, a fundraising director, could well be using video conferencing, 'talking to' his computer and using 'logic manager' to plan communications and fast track potential high value donors. All the technology required for this vision is available today but how effectively are fundraisers using it? More pragmatically, elsewhere in the same publication contributors John Rawlinson and Joe Saxton commented: 'Too many charity marketers still believe their business is fundraising. We believe this is an outdated view – that business is actually to create visions of a better world and to persuade people to support that vision by donating. It is about giving people the opportunity to make statements on who they are and what they believe in. It is about building the kind of relationship with them that enables them to further their dreams and feel good about it.' They go on to describe charity marketing as being in the 'Model T age.' Perhaps by now it's a Morris 1000 or even a Ford Escort but it still lags behind strong commercial models.

The challenge of the next decade will be to catch up and pass the 'designer models' of today. Organisations, both for-profit and not-for-profit, who integrate fully, plan and remain open to opportunities will succeed. Flexibility within well considered effective strategies will enable those best able to 'seize the day.'

Throughout this book an attempt has been made to keep language straightforward and provide detailed explanations for clarity only where the concepts may be unusual or somewhat technical. This should have made the argument accessible not just to any student of marketing but to anyone interested in developing and improving the reputation of their particular organisation – whether public, private, voluntary or social enterprise. The clearest conclusion is that for-profits and not-for-profits can work far more closely, creatively and beneficially. There is great profit and life enhancement in this route but it requires movement from both sides to make it a reality. That surely is an unbeatable proposition, partnership and marketing strategy.

# Sources of further help

' ... Five things everywhere under heaven constitutes perfect virtue; sincerity, gravity, generosity of soul, earnestness, and kindness.'
*Confucius*

'We need sincerity, if we can fake that we've got it made.'
*Groucho Marx*

**ACEVO** The Association of Chief Executives of Voluntary Organisations aims to improve standards of senior management in the sector and in particular improve development opportunities for chief executives. See *www.acevo.org.uk*

**ASA** Advertising Standards Association, the self- regulatory body that aims to ensure all advertising is legal, decent, honest and truthful. Advertisers agree to abide by a voluntary code of practice and be bound by the ASA's decisions. See *www.asa.org.uk*

**CAF** see p160 for further information.

**CIM** Chartered Institute of Marketing. The professional membership organisation for marketeers and marketing students. Source of excellent publications, training and research. CIM is the largest and most prestigious marketing association in the world and is the officially appointed body for setting the standards for sales and marketing professional development in the UK. The organisation is committed to delivering world-class support to equip marketeers with the knowledge and tools they need to stay ahead and excel in this challenging profession. See *www.cim.co.uk*

**CTT** Charity Technology Trust. Internet company set up by Peter Sweatman to help charities harness the power of the Internet for more cost-effective fundraising. See also Chapter seven and *www.ctt.org.uk*

**DSC** see p153 for further information.

**Fundraising UK** Internet site and organisation run by Howard Lake providing free news and information site for fundraisers working in the voluntary sector. As such it offers fundraisers and marketing professionals an extremely valuable information and research resource. See *www.fundraising.co.uk*

**Institute of Fundraising** see p162 for further information.

**NCVO** National Council of Voluntary Organisations is the campaigning umbrella organisation for the voluntary sector. A member organisation, it offers publications, research and training. See *www.ncvo.org.uk*

**RSA** Royal Society of Arts exists for the encouragement of the arts, manufacturing and commerce. The RSA, a charity, encourages the development of a principled, prosperous society and the release of human potential. With excellent facilities in London the organisation is membership based. See *www.rsa.org.uk*

**Westburn** are publishers of a number of marketing publications and have a very useful free online search facility for their 'Marketing Dictionary' and also for published articles around marketing issues. It is therefore a valuable glossary of marketing terminology and jargon. See *www.westburn.co.uk*

# References

Allford, Marion (1993) *Charity Appeals* London: J M Dent & Sons

Ansoff, Dr H Igor (1986) *Corporate Strategy* London: Penguin

Bruce, Ian (1998) *Successful Charity Marketing Meeting Need* London: ICSA Publishing

Baguley, John (2000) *Successful Fundraising* Stafford: Bibliotek Books

Burnett, Ken (2002) *Relationship Fundraising* San Franciso: Jossey-Bass

Central Office of Statistics (2002) Report on the 2001 census, London: HMSO

*Charity Awareness Monitor* (Feb 2002) London: The Future Foundation

Confucius (K'ung Fu-tzu) (551–479 BC) Chinese philosopher

Cram, Tony (2001) *Customers that Count* Harlow: Prentice Hall

Crossbow Research (May 2002) Market research budgets: Report on spend amounts of leading charities, London

de Bono, Edward (1981) *Atlas of Management Thinking* London: Maurice Temple Smith

*Dictionary of Business* (1996) Oxford: Oxford University Press

Direct Mail Information Service (2002) Annual report, London

Drummond, Graeme and Ensor, John (2001) *Strategic Marketing* Oxford: Butterworth Heinemann

Elcom Electronics (1986) Sales Literature for the Carphone Answering Machine

Fundratios (Dec 2001), Annual compilation – Centre for Interfirm Comparisons, Winchester

*From Mailshots to the Millennium* contributed volume (1995) London: Arts Publishing

HM Government (2002) Care Standards Act, London: HMSO London

Hewson, Anthony (Oct 1997) addressing Arthritis Care trustees, Blackpool

Karass, Chester (1970) *The Negotiating Game* New York: Thomas Y Crowell

Kotler, P and Fox, K F A (1985) *Strategic Marketing for Educational Institutions* New Jersey: Prentice Hall

Little, Leo T (1964) *Economics for Students* London: Jordan Publishing

Kay-Williams, Susan (2000) The five stages of fundraising: a framework for the development of fundraising, *International Journal of Nonprofit and Voluntary Sector Marketing* Vol. 5

McDonald, Malcolm (1984) *Marketing Plans: How to Prepare them, How to Use them* London: Heinemann

Mawson, Andrew (Nov 2002) Speaking at the CAF conference, London

Mitchell, Colin (Jan 2002) Selling the brand inside, *Harvard Business Review*

Morris, Richard (2000) *Cheshire the Man* London: Viking

Mullin, Redmond (2002) *Fundraising Strategy* London: CAF/ Institute of Fundraising

Ries, Al and Trout, Jack (1989) *Bottom up Marketing* New York: Magraw-Hill,

Rodgers, F G (1986) *The IBM Way* London: Guild Publishing

Sargeant, Adrian and Lee, Stephen (2003) *The Future of Giving* London: the Giving Campaign

Sargeant, Adrian (1998) *Marketing Management for Nonprofit Organisations* Oxford: Oxford University Press

Saxton, Joe (2002) *Polishing the Diamond* London: nfpSynergy

Searight, Sarah (1993) *Oasis* Calne, Wilts: Westernprint

Smyth, John (2002) *The Guide to UK Company Giving* London: DSC

Stapleton, John (1975) *Marketing* Sevenoaks: Hodder & Stoughton

*Third Sector* (17 July 2002) Quoting Charity Commission figures, London

Thirkettle, G L (1970) *Basic Economics* London: Macdonald & Evans

Von Clausewitz, Carl (1832) *On War* See Mullin

Willmott, Michael (2001) *Citizen Brands* Chichester: John Wiley & Sons

# About the Directory of Social Change

The Directory of Social Change (DSC) is an independent voice for positive social change, set up in 1975 to help voluntary organisations become more effective. It does this by providing practical, challenging and affordable information and training to meet the current, emerging and future needs of the sector.

DSC's main activities include:

- researching and publishing reference guides and handbooks;
- providing practical training courses;
- running conferences and briefing sessions;
- organising Charityfair, the biggest annual form for the sector;
- encouraging voluntary groups to network and share information;
- campaigning to promote the interests of the voluntary sector as a whole.

**The Directory of Social Change**

24 Stephenson Way
London
NW1 2DP

Federation House
Hope Street
Liverpool
L1 9BW
website: www.dsc.org.uk
e-mail: books@dsc.org.uk

*Publications and subscriptions*
tel: 020 7209 5151
fax: 020 7391 4804

*Publicity & Web Content*
tel: 020 7391 4900

*Policy & Research*
tel: 020 7391 4880
0151 708 0136

*Courses and conferences*
tel: 020 7209 4949
0151 708 0117

*Charityfair*
tel: 020 7391 4875
020 7209 1015 (exhibitors)

# Other publications from the Directory of Social Change

All the following titles are published by the Directory of Social Change, unless otherwise stated, and are available from:
Publications Department
Directory of Social Change
24 Stephenson Way
London
NW1 2DP

Call 020 7209 5151 or e-mail books@dsc.org.uk for more details and for a free books catalogue, which can also be viewed at the DSC website (www.dsc.org.uk).
Prices were correct at the time of going to press but may be subject to change.

## The fundraising series

**Published in association with CAF and the Institute of Fundraising.**

### Community Fundraising
*Edited by Harry Brown*

Volunteer networks are a key resource for fundraising, but are often not appreciated as they should be. This new title demonstrates how to make the most of your volunteers. It covers:

- what community fundraising is

- why people volunteer, the value of volunteers and staff attitudes to volunteers

- the recruitment, retention and development of volunteers

- the management of staff working with volunteers

- case studies from a range of different types of charities - and what can be learned from these.

192 pages, 1st edition, 2002

ISBN 1 900360 98 5 £19.95

## Corporate Fundraising

*Edited by Valerie Morton*

Corporate Fundraising is a fast-moving area and the second edition of this book has been completely revised and updated to include:

- new chapters on corporate social responsibility and on evaluation
- a new appendix on the internet
- a revised section on the legal and tax framework
- a range of new case studies from major charities and companies such as NCH, Diabetes UK, One2One and the Mencap-Transco partnership.

The book continues to offer a comprehensive overview, detailing the variety of ways in which charities and companies may work together to mutual advantage, and addressing key issues around ethics and standards.

200 pages, 2nd edition, 2002

ISBN 1 903991 00 5 £19.95

## Fundraising Databases

*Peter Flory*

Computerised databases are an essential tool for fundraising, but fundraisers often lack the technical background to help them choose a suitable database and use it effectively. This new book provides a clear framework for making and implementing such decisions. It explains what a database is and how it works, before going on to examine:

- why fundraisers need a database
- the functions of a fundraising database
- future trends

Case studies from a range of charities are used throughout to illustrate the points made.

160 pages, 1st edition, 2001

ISBN 1 900360 91 8 £19.95

## Fundraising Strategy

*Redmond Mullin*

The key to successful fundraising is rigorous strategic planning and this influential title has become essential reading for all serious fundraisers, as a background to the whole series. The second edition draws on some more recent examples, such as the NSPCC Full

Stop campaign, to further clarify the principles and process of strategy and demonstrate its place in fundraising campaigns. The book:

- discusses the concept of strategy and its relevance to not-for-profit bodies
- outlines the planning process for designing and implementing the strategy
- provides case studies of different strategies in different types and sizes of funding programmes
- has been fully updated to take into account important changes in areas such as the tax regime and the National Lottery.

160 pages, 2nd edition, 2002

ISBN 1 903991 22 6 £19.95

## Legacy Fundraising
## The Art of Seeking Bequests

*Edited by Sebastian Wilberforce*

This unique guide to one of the most important sources of revenue for charities has been revised and updated to include new material on telephone fundraising, forecasting income, and profiling. It also contains the full text of the new Institute of Fundraising Code of Practice on legacy fundraising. Contributions from a range of experts in the field cover both strategy and techniques, and are complemented by perspectives from donors and their families. The breadth of coverage and accessible style ensure that, whether you are an established legacy fundraiser or new to the field, this book is a must.

224 pages, 2nd edition, 2001

ISBN 1 900360 93 4 £19.95

## Trust Fundraising

*Edited by Anthony Clay*

This book outlines a variety of approaches to trusts that will save trustees' time and ensure greater success for fundraising by:

- emphasising the importance of research and maintaining records;
- demonstrating the value of using contacts and a personal approach;
- reinforcing the need for detailed planning of a strategy;
- showing how to make an approach to trusts, and how not to;
- stressing the importance of continued contact with a trust.

152 pages, 1st edition, 1999

ISBN 1 85934 069 5 £19.95

# Other titles from DSC

### The Complete Fundraising Handbook

*Nina Botting & Michael Norton*

Published in association with the Institute of Fundraising

For the new edition of this ever-popular title, the information has been completely updated and also reorganised, making it even easier to use. It is now divided into three parts, covering:

- fundraising principles and strategies
- sources of fundraising – including individual donors, grant-making trusts, companies, and central and local government
- fundraising techniques – from house-to-house collections and challenge events, to direct mail and capital appeals.

Illustrated with case studies throughout, the book provides a wealth of practical advice on every aspect of fundraising for charity.

416 pages, 4th edition, 2001

ISBN 1 900360 84 5 £16.95

### Promoting your Cause
### A Guide for Fundraisers and Campaigners

*Karen Gilchrist*

This new title is brimful of ideas to raise the profile of your organisation, establish a positive reputation, increase awareness of your cause and communicate effectively with your target audience. It covers:

- defining your audience
- printed material
- websites
- video and audio
- using the media
- open days, road shows and exhibitions
- making a presentation
- merchandise
- creative packages
- tracking your progress and planning ahead
- 128 pages, 1st edition, 2002

ISBN 1 900360 95 0 £10.95

## The Grant-making Trusts CD-ROM

*Software development by Funderfinder*

Published in association with CAF

This CD-ROM combines the trusts databases of the Directory of Social Change and the Charities Aid Foundation to provide the most comprehensive and up-to-date information ever on grant-making trusts. The improved search facilities ensure fast, easy and effective searching across the whole database.

*Contents*

- Around 4,000 trusts as listed in the *Directory of Grant Making Trusts 2003/2004*, the three *Guides to Major Trusts 2003/2004* and 2002/2003, the four *Guides to Local Trusts 2002/2003*, and the *Guide to Scottish Trusts 2002/2003*

- Full commentary from DSC guide displayed if available

- *DGMT* entry displayed for smaller trusts where full commentary is unavailable.

*Search facilities*

- Powerful combined search by geographical area, type of activity and type of beneficiary

- Search by name of trust, location, type of grant or trustee

- Search by key word.

*Software*

- PC format only

- Runs on Windows 95 and above

- Network capability

- 'Getting started' tutorial

- Hyperlinks to trust websites

- Facility to bookmark selected trusts, add your own notes, print individual entries and tag contact details and addresses for export.

Single CD-ROM, 3rd edition, 2003

ISBN 1 903991 32 3 £115 + VAT = £135.13

£85 + VAT = £99.88 for existing users

### Website: trustfunding.org.uk

*www.trustfunding.org.uk* contains all the same data as the *Grant-making Trusts CD-ROM*, but will be regularly updated throughout the year.

■ Search on geographical area, type of activity or type of beneficiary; by name of trust, name of trustee, type of grant, or location; key word search.

■ Browser requirements: Internet Explorer version 4 and above or Netscape version 4 and above.

■ Hyperlinks to trust websites or e-mail.

■ Facility to print individual trust records and tag contact and address details for export.

*Annual subscription*

Charities and voluntary organisations: £115 + VAT = £135.13

Statutory and commercial organisations: £160 + VAT = £188

Register using a user name and password of your choice. You can then log on to the site as often as you wish for the duration of your subscription.

### The Complete Guide to Business & Strategic Planning For Voluntary Organisations

*Alan Lawrie*

This best-selling management title has been fully revised and updated, drawing on the greater experience of business planning that many voluntary organisations now have. A solid business plan is an essential requirement for applications to key funders such as the National Lottery, and managers increasingly recognise the importance of strategic planning to the effectiveness of their organisation. Features of this edition include:

■ new exercises, activities and case studies

■ more coverage of how funders see and use business plans

■ additional material on the context and process of business planning

■ larger A4 format to better accommodate the exercises and templates.

96 pages, 2nd edition, 2001

ISBN 1 900360 87 X £12.50

# About CAF

CAF, Charities Aid Foundation, is a registered charity with a unique mission – to increase the substance of charity in the UK and overseas. It provides services that are both charitable and financial which help donors make the most of their giving and charities make the most of their resources.

As an integral part of its activities, CAF works to raise standards of management in voluntary organisations. This includes the making of grants by its own Grants Council, sponsorship of the Charity Annual Report and Accounts Awards, seminars, training courses and the Charities Annual Conference, the largest regular gathering of key people from within the voluntary sector. In addition, Charitynet (www.charitynet.org) is now established as the leading Internet site on voluntary action.

For decades, CAF has led the way in developing tax-effective services to donors, and these are now used by more than 250,000 individuals and 2,000 of the UK's leading companies, between them giving £150 million each year to charity. Many are also using CAF's CharityCard, the world's first debit card designed exclusively for charitable giving. CAF's unique range of investment and administration services for charities includes the CafCash High Interest Cheque Account, two common investment funds for longer-term investment and a full appeals and subscription management service.

CAF's activities are not limited to the UK, however. Increasingly, CAF is looking to apply the same principles and develop similar services internationally, in its drive to increase the substance of charity across the world. CAF has offices and sister organisations in the United States, Bulgaria, South Africa, Russia, India and Brussels.

CAF Research is a leading source of information and research on the voluntary sector's income and resources. Its annual publication, Dimensions of the Voluntary Sector, provides year-on-year updates and its Research Report series covers a wide range of topics, including costs benchmarking, partnership resources, and trust and company funding. More details on research and publications may be found on www.CAFonline.org/research

For more information about CAF, please visit www.CAFonline.org/

# About the Institute of Fundraising

The Institute of Fundraising is the only organisation that exists to represent and support the professional interests of fundraisers at all levels. The Institute of Fundraising welcomes membership applications from all those working in a fundraising role or consultancy practice – from those new to the profession to those with many years' experience.

The benefits to be gained are available to all. As a professional body, the Institute of Fundraising assists its members at every stage and in every facet of their professional development. It provides opportunities for continuing professional education, a forum for discussion on issues of common concern, a source of information and a point of contact with other professionals.

The Institute of Fundraising Certificate of Membership is evidence of the holder's commitment to the Codes and the professional standards set by the Institute. Since membership is individual, it is fully transferable if you change your job. In liaison with other umbrella groups, the Institute of Fundraising also represents members' interests to charities, government, the media and to the public.

The Institute of Fundraising is supported financially by many charities who recognise the importance and needs of the organisation, having become affiliates of its Charitable Trust. Fundraising staff of these affiliated charities enjoy reduced subscription fees. Through its members, the Institute of Fundraising liaises worldwide with allied organisations, such as the National Society of Fundraising Executives in the USA and the Australian Institute of Fundraising, and is represented on the World Fundraising Council.

The Institute of Fundraising aims, through its Trust, to further knowledge, skills and effectiveness in the field of fundraising. It serves the interests of its members, the professional fundraisers, and through them, the interests of charitable bodies and donors.

The Institute of Fundraising aims to set and develop standards of fundraising practice which encompass:

- growth in the funds and resources available for charitable expenditure;
- thorough knowledge of proven fundraising techniques;
- new fundraising opportunities;
- cost effectiveness;
- strict adherence to the law;
- accountability.

# Institute of Fundraising Codes of Practice, Guidance Notes, and the Charity Donors' Rights Charter

The Institute of Fundraising Codes of Practice and Guidance Notes aim to act as a guide to best practice for fundraisers, and as a benchmark against which the public can measure fundraising practice. They cover a wide variety of issues and aim to address both practical and ethical concerns.

The Codes are drawn up by working parties composed of representatives of the various interested constituents in a particular field, and undergo an extensive consultation process through the charities affiliated to the Institute of Fundraising, regulators and government.

As new areas of interest are identified, so new Codes are drafted, often at the rate of two or three each year, under the supervision of the Institute of Fundraising Standards Committee. Both Charity Commission and Home Office are represented on this committee and play a major role in the development of any new work.

The Codes are endorsed and observed by fundraising organisations throughout the UK. They are recognised as demonstrating the commitment of the voluntary sector to the promotion of best practice.

The Charity Donors' Rights Charter has been developed as a compact between fundraisers and the supporters of the organisations for which they work. It aims to address the expectations that a supporter has of the organisation they give to, and to articulate the commitment the sector makes to them.

## Codes of Practice

Charity Challenge Events
UK Charity Challenge Events
Fundraising in Schools
House to House Collections
Telephone Recruitment of Collectors
Personal Solicitation of Committed Gifts

Legacy Fundraising
Outbound Telephone Support
Payroll Giving
Reciprocal Charity Mailings

## Guidance Notes

The Acceptance and Refusal of Donations
Data Protection Act 1998
The Management of Static Collection Boxes
The Use of Chain Letters as a Fundraising Technique
UK Charity Challenge Events

## New Codes for 2001

Raffles and Lotteries
Fundraising on the Internet

Copies of the Codes of Practice, Guidance Notes and Charity Donors' Rights Charter may be obtained from the Institute of Fundraising at:

Institute of Fundraising
5th Floor
Market Towers
1 Nine Elms Lane
London SW8 5NQ
Tel: 020 7627 3436

Or from:
enquiries@institute-of-fundraising.org.uk

# Index